T<small>RUE</small> W<small>ORSHIP</small>

T<small>RADITIONAL</small>. C<small>ONTEMPORARY</small>. B<small>IBLICAL</small>.

D<small>AVID</small> W<small>HITCOMB</small>
& M<small>ARK</small> W<small>ARD</small>, S<small>R</small>.

A<small>MBASSADOR</small> I<small>NTERNATIONAL</small>
Greenville, South Carolina • Belfast, Northern Ireland

True Worship

Cover design & page layout by A & E Media—Paula Shepherd

ISBN 1 932307 30 3

Published by the Ambassador Group

Ambassador Emerald International
427 Wade Hampton Blvd.
Greenville, SC 29609
USA
www.emeraldhouse.com

and

Ambassador Publications Ltd.
Providence House
Ardenlee Street
Belfast BT6 8QJ
Northern Ireland
www.ambassador-productions.com

The colophon is a trademark of Ambassador

TRUE WORSHIP

To our wives,
who fear the Lord
and shall be praised

TRUE WORSHIP IS ACCEPTABLE TO GOD
BECAUSE IT COMES FROM A RIGHTEOUS HEART.

⸖

TRUE WORSHIP PLEASES GOD
BECAUSE IT IS SACRIFICIAL.

⸖

TRUE WORSHIP REQUIRES FAITH THAT
OBEYS GOD AND TRUSTS HIS WORD.

⸖

TRUE WORSHIP ACKNOWLEDGES THAT GOD
SOVEREIGNLY CHOOSES TO BE LOYAL TO HIS PEOPLE.

⸖

TRUE WORSHIP UNDERSTANDS THAT GOD
IS FAITHFUL TO HIS PROMISES.

⸖

TRUE WORSHIP REQUIRES SEPARATION
FROM FALSE WORSHIP.

⸖

TRUE WORSHIP IS CENTERED ON GOD'S WORD
AND IS ONLY FOR THOSE WHO BELIEVE THAT WORD.

⸖

TRUE WORSHIP FLOWS FROM OBEDIENCE
AND LEADS TO FAITHFUL SERVICE.

⸖

TRUE WORSHIP REQUIRES COMPLETE COMMITMENT
AND A WILLINGNESS TO GIVE EVERYTHING TO GOD.

TRUE WORSHIP REQUIRES A BROKEN HEART
THAT HAS REPENTED FROM SIN.

———◆———

TRUE WORSHIP HAS INTEGRITY BECAUSE
IT RELIES ON GOD RATHER THAN MAN.

———◆———

TRUE WORSHIP IS EXCITING WHEN IT IS ROOTED
IN A PROPER FEAR OF AND REVERENCE FOR GOD.

———◆———

TRUE WORSHIP PROMOTES A PROPER
UNDERSTANDING OF GOD'S WORD.

———◆———

TRUE WORSHIP EXALTS GOD
FOR HIS HOLINESS.

———◆———

TRUE WORSHIP IS CHARACTERIZED
BY HUMILITY BEFORE GOD.

———◆———

TRUE WORSHIP TRUSTS GOD AND DESIRES
HIS WAY RATHER THAN OUR OWN.

———◆———

TRUE WORSHIP PUTS GOD BEFORE
THE TRADITIONS OF MEN.

———◆———

TRUE WORSHIP MAINTAINS A RIGHT BALANCE
BETWEEN INTELLECT AND EMOTION.

TRUE WORSHIP CAN BE PRACTICED ONLY
BY THOSE WHO TRULY KNOW GOD.

TRUE WORSHIP BOASTS IN CHRIST ALONE
AND NOT IN HUMAN ACHIEVEMENTS.

TRUE WORSHIP GIVES ALL GLORY TO GOD AND
THEREFORE REQUIRES SUBMISSION TO HIM.

TRUE WORSHIP EXPRESSES COMPLETE FAITH
IN THE GOD WHO IS THE OBJECT OF THAT FAITH.

TRUE WORSHIP BOWS BEFORE THE GOD WHO
IS CREATOR AND SUSTAINER OF ALL THINGS.

TRUE WORSHIP BOWS BEFORE THE LAMB WHO
HAS REDEEMED US FROM CONDEMNATION.

TRUE WORSHIP REJOICES IN GOD'S TRIUMPH AND THE
COMING COMPLETION OF HIS REDEMPTIVE PLAN.

TRUE WORSHIP PRAISES GOD FOR HIS
RIGHTEOUS JUDGMENT AGAINST SIN.

TRUE WORSHIP JOYOUSLY ANTICIPATES
THE IMMINENT RETURN OF CHRIST.

TABLE OF CONTENTS

FOREWORD

If we define worship as anything that happens inside a church, then worship is easy to understand. But of course, the issue is not that simple. What *is* worship? In the midst of today's often contentious debate, what the Church needs, clearly, is a refreshing return to Scripture itself for a recovery of the biblical ideals for authentic worship. Such a return to biblical ideals is what I have discovered in reading *True Worship*.

What strikes one immediately is the "scripturalness" of this book. *True Worship* is permeated with the Bible, not merely through occasional quotations but with sustained exposition. Nearly every page is focused on the actual text of the Word of God. But even beyond this pervasive attention to Scripture, the book *leads* with the Bible. The authors do not begin with personal conclusions and then attempt to justify them scripturally. Instead, *True Worship* starts with the Bible passages themselves, then draws the conclusions that surface inevitably, almost seamlessly, from a proper understanding of those texts.

That is another outstanding feature of *True Worship*. The applications come so naturally. They are not forced. When the reader follows the exposition he or she is led, naturally and without contrivance, to an almost immediate grasp of the biblical principles. Such qualities are a mark of both expositional integrity and pastoral wisdom.

The latter quality, too, bears explanation. *True Worship* conveys a message that, clearly, was conceived in the heart of a skillful, caring pastor. In the capable hands of David Whitcomb and co-author Mark Ward, the book retains a scholarly authority, yet obviously is aimed at readers who sit in pews rather than in classrooms. It is a book for

Worship that God Accepts

Cain and Abel • Genesis 4:1-15

Abel also brought of the firstborn of his flock and of their fat.
And the Lord respected Abel and his offering,

Many people would consider my Southern town to be the buckle of the Bible Belt. Each week our city paper runs a full-page profile about a local pastor and his congregation. Not long ago, a report about worship practices in local churches made the front page of the city section. A blizzard of letters-to-the-editor followed, some positive and others sharply negative in their response to the coverage. "This newspaper," an editorial column later explained, "has described the attempts by some faith communities to offer more 'contemporary' worship as a way to break down barriers that keep persons from our churches." After surveying readers' reactions the editorial concluded, "No wonder some writers have said that Christians are in the midst of 'worship wars' these days!"

It seems that every denomination, sect, and congregation today is mired in this quandary. Who is right? Is it right to have contemporary worship services in order to attract younger people or those who are unchurched or unsaved? Is it right to maintain conservative, traditional types of worship in order to please older members and other people who think that God's holiness is thereby reflected? Do both sides have valid points to make?

I had a friend in the ministry who came to the conclusion that both sides do have valid viewpoints. He decided to try to meet the needs that he perceived in his church by offering each Sunday an early-morning country and western service, a late-morning traditional service, and a contemporary service at night. After a year or two, however, his church shattered and split into different factions.

If trying to please everyone's taste is unworkable, what is workable? Is there really a right way and a wrong way to worship? Another way to phrase that question is this: since worship has to do with God, should we therefore expect that God, in His Word, has given His people enough evidence to learn what He is like, what He expects, what He desires, and how His creation can please Him through worship? I believe the answer is yes!

Do I believe that the Bible spells out the order of service that God expects? Of course not. But the Scriptures do provide a wealth of examples, illustrations, and instructions regarding what constitutes proper worship to the one true God. It promises such a wealth of instructions, in fact, that I believe any Christian can confidently know there is a right way to worship God according to the Bible. Our task is to discover that kind of "true" worship and do it!

TWO DIFFERENT KINDS OF HEARTS

A good place to begin the study of worship is with the first example of worship found in the Bible, the story of Cain and Abel. In this account we learn that these two sons of Adam and Eve were different, not only in age and occupation, but also in character.

A reading of Genesis 4 reveals that Abel was a submissive shepherd. This fact in itself, however, did not give him any natural advantage with God over his brother. Abel did not please God more simply because he was a keeper of sheep and Cain was a tiller of the soil. Yet shepherding was Abel's chosen profession, a choice that was based probably on a desire and ability to work with animals. It seems likely that Abel was quite satisfied that shepherding placed him in God's will.

What is obvious from Genesis 4 is that Abel understood God's requirements regarding sacrifices and offerings. "And the LORD respected Abel and his offering" (4:4). When it was time for him to bring an offering to God, it appears there was no argument from him. That unquestioning spirit is a trait found among those who are submissive to God's will and purposes. Abel appeared to be submissive even to his older brother when Abel went to the field, apparently at Cain's suggestion, and without offering an argument. "Now Cain talked with Abel his brother: and it came to pass, when they were in the field, that Cain rose up against Abel his brother and killed him" (4:8).

In contrast to Abel, Cain was a stubborn farmer. That is not to disparage farmers! When it came to pleasing God, Cain was not at a disadvantage simply because of his occupation. Farming was then, as it is now, good and honest work. Where would the world be without farmers? Amos, one of God's chief prophets, was a farmer. God certainly did not condemn Cain for his line of work.

Indeed, it seems reasonable to assume that Cain was equal to Abel in his knowledge of God's requirements for offerings and sacrifices. But instead of submitting to God's parameters regarding his offerings, Cain chose to do his own thing in his own way.

How do we know this? The New Testament clearly sets forth the distinctions between Cain and Abel. Jesus once taught about Abel when He was involved in a discussion with the Pharisees. They and their forefathers, Jesus stated, were guilty of shedding the blood of the prophets whom God had sent.

> Therefore, indeed, I send you prophets, wise men, and scribes: some of them you will kill and crucify...from the blood of righteous Abel to the blood of Zechariah. (Matt. 23:34-35)

Within this passage, therefore, Jesus declares that Abel was one of the prophets. That meant that Abel had received God's words and was responsible to declare those words. Furthermore, Jesus described Abel as a righteous prophet, which meant that he was living in a right relationship with God. When a servant of God has a heart that is right before God, he will prove it by living rightly in the midst of his crooked and perverse generation. Christ affirmed that Abel lived as a godly example before his brother Cain.

The writer to the Hebrews states, "By faith Abel offered to God a more excellent sacrifice than Cain, through which he obtained witness that he was righteous" (Heb. 11:4). What did the author mean by saying that Abel operated according to faith? This is an affirmation that Abel exercised faith in what he knew about God, and that he did so not only in daily life but specifically when it came time to express worship. In his worship Abel offered a sacrifice that was excellent, which means that it was full or complete when measured against God's requirements. Such action served as a witness to the fact that he was righteous.

The New Testament expands our knowledge of Cain, also, by stating that he had an evil heart.

> In this the children of God and the children of the devil are manifest: Whoever does not practice righteousness is not of God, nor is he who does not love his brother. For this is the message that you heard from the beginning, that we should love one another, not as Cain who was of the wicked one and murdered his brother. And why did he murder him? Because his works were evil and his brother's righteous. (1 John 3:10-12)

Cain worshiped the way he did because he had a heart that was predisposed to oppose God. Why would a person with a contrary heart engage in worship at all? Cain's condition certainly stood as a contrast to Abel's righteous heart. Abel illustrated righteousness but Cain typified rebellion. Thus Jude writes, condemning rebellious teachers, "Woe to them! For they have gone in the way of Cain" (Jude 11). Cain did not hesitate to do something religious, but his heart was far removed from God.

TWO DIFFERENT KINDS OF WORSHIP

Even though their outward expressions of worship seemed very similar, Cain and Abel offered different expressions of worship—because their hearts were different. Of course, it was to be expected that the outward expressions of their worship would be similar, since both men were aware of God's requirements. Both men brought their offerings to God at a set time, for example. "And in the process of time it came to pass, that Cain brought an offering of the fruit of the ground to the Lord" (Gen. 4:3).

Here, the Hebrew words translated "in the process of time" literally mean "at the end of time." What was that end? Maybe it referred to a thanksgiving offering that God prescribed at the end of the year or at the end of harvest in order to call man's attention to God's goodness. Maybe the phrase points to the end of the week, a Sabbath that commemorated God's day of rest after six days of creation. We do not know from this text what "end" God meant. Yet God has the prerogative to set a time when His creatures express worship to Him. Cain and Abel were both aware of this prerogative, for they engaged in worship at the same time.

Cain and Abel also engaged in worship in the same *place*. The words "brought...an offering unto the Lord" probably indicate a specified location. Maybe God required Cain and Abel to bring the offerings to that spot at the east of Eden where God had set the cherubim with the flaming swords (Gen. 3:24). Maybe God instructed Cain and Abel to bring their offerings to a place where His *shekinah* glory dwelt, much as it did in later years when God's presence was in Moses' tabernacle and Solomon's temple. God has the prerogative to set both a time and a place for worship.

Furthermore, both Cain and Abel were engaged in acts of *worship*—not necessarily in sacrifices for sin. The offerings that God later prescribed under the Levitical system could express thanksgiving, repentance, or praise, which are all expressions of worship. The simple action of presenting an offering implies bowing down before the mighty God to express submission or obedience. At least outwardly, Cain and Abel appeared to be doing the same thing. Yet beyond the apparent similarities, Cain and Abel were actually quite different in their expressions of worship.

This distinction is an important one, and it applies to everything we see in the world of religion today. Not all expressions of worship are truly worship. Abel's worship proved that he had a heart of submission to the Lord: he understood God's words and trusted them, and he acknowledged God's authority to prescribe worship. He also expressed his submission by giving God the best he had to offer. "Abel also brought of the firstborn of his flock and of their fat" (Gen. 4:4). Those terms always indicate a sacrifice of the best.

By contrast, Cain's worship was empty and self-centered. He knew God's requirements and he did what God required him to do—but no more. "Cain brought an offering of the fruit of the ground to the LORD... but [the LORD] did not respect Cain and his offering" (4:3, 5). Fruit was an acceptable offering, but notice the glaring omission. The text does not say that Cain, as compared to Abel, offered his first or his best fruit.

Does this observation constitute an argument from silence? I do not think so. The Hebrew word *minkawh* is used in Genesis 4 for both Cain's and Abel's offerings. This word is very common in the Old Testament and appears nearly two hundred times. Sometimes the word refers to gifts that friends exchange with each other, but in the vast majority of references the word speaks of the grain offerings that God required within the Mosaic law. From the Hebrew text alone we cannot say that Cain's offering of grain was inherently less acceptable than Abel's blood offering. The difference lay not in the *offering* but rather in the *offerers*.

GOD ACCEPTS ONLY TRUE WORSHIP

What was the difference? Cain and Abel worshiped at the same time, at the same place, and through the same outward actions. But God "had respect" for Abel's expression of worship; the phrase means that He regarded it favorably and accepted it kindly. In other words, God was *predisposed* toward the kind of worship Abel offered. God's acceptance of Abel's offering proved that Abel's worship was true.

However, God "did not respect" Cain's expression of worship. Why not? What was wrong with Cain's worship?

Cain proved by his response to God's disapproval that his heart was not right before God. When God disapproved of his worship style, "Cain was very angry, and his countenance fell" (Gen. 4:5). He did not ask forgiveness or accept correction. Instead, he took his anger out on his brother, whose righteousness highlighted his own unrighteousness.

Does that reaction sound familiar in our "worship wars" of today? When God disapproves of us for any reason, we have the ability to accept His correction humbly. Instead, though, we often decide that being angry with our brother is "justifiable" on some basis. That attitude characterized Cain's heart, and it became obvious in his worship.

Cain became angry, and then he compounded his problems by refusing to do well. "If you do well, will you not be accepted?" the Lord asked; "and if you do not do well, sin lies at the door" (4:7). Doing well was the whole issue. When God rebukes us, as He did Cain, for failing to have a right heart in worship, we still have the opportunity to do good. God challenged Cain to that end, but Cain was not interested. Instead of dealing with the sin that expressed itself in false worship, he refused to acknowledge his error. That refusal led him into a downward spiral until he committed the ultimate sin of the flesh—murder.

In this downward cycle Cain illustrated some common traits of stubborn sinners: denying his error (4:7), playing the hypocrite (4:8), and refusing to confess his sin when confronted (4:9). He complained about God's law (4:13) then criticized God Himself (4:14), even as God continued to show mercy (4:15). How longsuffering our God is as He warns, chides, and rebukes us in an effort to draw us into a correct relationship with Him.

As the examples of Cain and Abel teach us, true worship is expressed by those who have righteous hearts. Such righteous hearts are most obvious, however, in the circumstances of life that precede and follow the worship itself. In other words, a person who proves his love for the things of the world on Monday through Saturday probably does not engage in true worship on Sunday. True worship comes instead from a heart that not only knows what is recorded in the Bible, but also trusts in and submits to God and His Word.

THINGS TO THINK ABOUT

1. Do you think it is possible to know from the Bible whether there is a right way and a wrong way to worship God?

2. How did Abel's life show a submissive heart toward God? How did Cain's life show a lack of submission?

3. What does the New Testament teach us about Abel and Cain?

4. Abel and Cain both worshiped at the same time and place, and outwardly performed similar acts. Why did God accept the worship of one and not the other?

5. How did Cain respond to God's disapproval? What can you learn from his example?

Worship That Pleases God

Noah • Genesis 8:20-22

*Then Noah built an altar to the Lord, and took of every clean animal
and of every clean bird, and offered burnt offerings on the altar.*

N early every fast food restaurant today has a "value menu."
These menus contain items that do not cost much, with
a wide selection of choices for every taste. Although its
nutritional content may be limited, the menu is designed for people who
feel hungry but do not want to spend much time or money on food.

Of course, you can see where I am going with this picture. The
church in America today is characterized by a vast proliferation of
choices. A typical large suburban church offers a wide menu of youth
groups, care groups, and support groups, as well as activities from
aerobic exercise to recreational basketball. Many churches take a similar
approach to worship, too, combining contemporary and traditional
elements, or offering separate worship services in each style.

My point here is not to say that a particular church program or
practice is wrong. A desire to help people at their point of need should
characterize every church that honors the Word of God. Nevertheless, an
atmosphere has arisen today in which, given all the options available, most
Americans choose a church based on whether it meets their felt needs and
preferences. In turn, a growing number of churches are reevaluating their
programs with the expressed intention of attracting more people.

This picture is far different than the once-familiar concept of church as a little band of followers who meet together for a time of solemn prayer. Is one concept right and the other wrong? Are both right? Can anyone claim to know the pattern for "true" worship when the contrasts are so great?

What seems clear is that a growing number of Americans are practicing a kind of "value-menu Christianity." They feel hungry but, in their hurry to get somewhere else, choose only a quick bite of so-called worship that does not cost them much. As a result of their choice, they become spiritually weak and under-nourished. That spiritual weakening can easily happen to you or me. As Christians we face the same demands and pressures, as well as the same allurements and enticements, as do non-Christian people. When something has got to give, the commitment to worship our God can suffer.

What can we do? We must derive our patterns and practices of worship—all of them—from the teaching and examples in God's Word. We must compile the examples and the plain instruction of Scripture and then determine the most reverent way to express our love, thanksgiving, and devotion to God. When our worship is based on the *fact* of God's Word, then we have a foundation to stand upon even when our *feelings* fluctuate.

WORSHIP BEGINS WITH THE FEAR OF GOD

The first recorded example of worship in the Bible is that of Abel and Cain. The second is that of Noah.

In Genesis 8:20 we read that Noah walked out of the ark, built an altar, and worshiped God. Why? The Bible does not give a specific reason for Noah's action. But common sense dictates that Noah's immediate circumstances instilled the fear of God in him. He had just survived the greatest cataclysm in the history of mankind. He had been through an amazing sequence of events that left an indelible image of God's power stamped on his mind.

Many years earlier, God had revealed to this man His will about the flood of destruction, the ark, and the salvation of his family. Why did God choose to reveal His will to Noah? Noah must have wondered why God chose him, but he obeyed God's word. He spent much of his life building a structure that made no sense to him or to his incredulous neighbors. The writer to the Hebrews recorded that

> By faith Noah, being divinely warned of things not yet seen, moved with godly fear, prepared an ark for the saving of his household, by which he condemned the world and became heir of the righteousness which is according to faith. (Heb. 11:7)

This man of faith must have marveled when it came time to load up the ark. Where did the animals come from? How did they know that they should come to the ark? How did they know where the ark was? Apparently, God brought the animals to Noah. Then over the next few months Noah witnessed with his five senses the absolute destruction of all life forms from the entire earth. It was phenomenal! Mind-boggling! What a mighty God who could do such work!

Noah was right to fear God in response to this display of power. Yet Noah had respected God even before God had fully demonstrated His power. From the outset, Noah had done all that God commanded him (Gen. 7:5), even though men must have ridiculed and resisted him. While the scoffers jeered, Noah trusted God. Noah completed God's will because he feared God instead of man. As a result of his fear of God, he saw the mass destruction that befell his accusers and he experienced God's hand of deliverance. What did Noah see when he walked out of the ark? How did Noah feel? It is no wonder that he feared God.

Many of us who attend church services in America today have never experienced God's deliverance from destruction. We do not know the power of God to deliver because, in our affluence, we have gone to great lengths to insulate ourselves from trouble. After all, who wants to face uncomfortable circumstances? Why undergo a trial if it can be avoided? The American way is the easy way, the happy way.

Yet it is possible for every person to understand, from firsthand experience, the power of God to deliver from destruction. We understand that power when we are born again and delivered by God from sin and hell. Sadly, there are people who go to church and are "religious" but who have not been born again. Not having experienced God's power to save, they cannot know the kind of reverence that comes from godly fear. "Our evangelical culture tends to take the awesome reality of a transcendent God who is worthy to be feared," observes one Christian leader, "and downsize Him so He can fit into our 'buddy system.'"

WORSHIP INVOLVES SACRIFICE

Noah worshiped God because he feared God. The Genesis story indicates that the first thing Noah did when he walked out of the ark was to build an altar to the Lord. But notice that there is no indication that God commanded Noah to build an altar and make a sacrifice.

> So Noah went out, and...built an altar to the LORD, and took of every clean animal and of every clean bird, and offered burnt offerings on the altar. (Gen. 8:18-20)

Why was building an altar Noah's first act upon leaving the ark? Was he following a religious tradition that he believed was expected of him? No, the most reasonable explanation is that Noah, having been delivered from certain destruction, was motivated to worship God by a sincere desire. This explanation is especially probable in light of what Noah did next.

On the altar he built, Noah sacrificed living animals. The text states that his offering of thanksgiving to God consisted of every kind of "clean" animal and every kind of "clean" bird. That statement is an interesting one. Not until hundreds of years later, in the time of Moses, did God incorporate into Israel's sacrificial system a distinction between clean and unclean animals. So what was Noah doing, centuries earlier, by sacrificing only "clean" animals?

Remember that Noah took on to the ark two of each kind of unclean animal, but *seven* of each clean animal. It seems likely that the term "clean animal" is a reference to animals that could be domesticated. In later years, the "clean" animals needed for sacrifices were taken from domesticated herds. Therefore, when God commanded Noah to take an extra number of clean animals, it seems He was preparing to sustain Noah's family with those animals after the flood. The next chapter, of the Bible contains God's command that allowed the eating of animals for the first time. So although the clean animals played a vital role in the sustaining of his family, Noah gladly sacrificed them in the process of worshiping God.

His example stands in stark contrast to the practice of our own day, when so many Christians prefer worship of convenience, worship that meets their needs but demands nothing from them. We even schedule worship services so that they do not interfere with outside activities. The old idea of attending church "whenever the doors are open" is considered unrealistic in our society. With all the demands and pressures of modern life, can we really expect people to be at church for every service?

It is at this point that "value-menu Christianity" may be at odds with the example of Noah. The admitted purpose of some worship practices is to draw people who may feel more comfortable in a service that reflects their preferences. Am I suggesting that churches should never consciously attempt to be relevant to those in the pews? Of course not. We owe our English Bible, for example, to men who desired to make the Scriptures more accessible for ordinary people.

But when our worship services—their music, their format, and even their message—are driven by human preferences, have we failed the test of true worship? Noah worshiped out of a heart that feared the awesome power of God and was thankful for deliverance from destruction. Then he demonstrated his attitude through worship in which he sacrificed something of himself. Are we doing the same in our own worship?

WORSHIP COMES FROM EXPERIENCING GRACE

The fact that God was satisfied with Noah's sacrifice unfolds a picture of His great grace. The account of Noah's sacrifice states that it pleased God, for "the LORD smelled a soothing aroma" (Gen. 8:21). Noah's sacrifice might point toward God's future requirement, under Mosaic law, for thanksgiving offerings and sin offerings to be burnt offerings. But it is certainly a picture that points a long way through time to the future sacrifice of Christ, which is the only sacrifice that pleases God for eternity. For Noah offered his sacrifice against a backdrop of destruction that God sent because of man's terrible sinfulness.

Thus, in stating that God smelled the aroma from the sacrifice and was pleased, the account certainly speaks of something more than just smoke in God's nostrils. It speaks of the whole person of Noah that was involved in worship. God saw the evidence of Noah's heart of obedience all through his experience with the ark. He saw Noah's fear. He heard Noah's prayers. And God was pleased. He accepted this expression of worship. In light of His satisfaction God promised,

> I will never again curse the ground for man's sake, although the imagination of man's heart is evil from his youth; nor will I again destroy every living thing as I have done. (Gen. 8:21)

But this promise must be understood in light of all the Scriptures. When God said that He would never curse the ground again, He was not promising to remove the curse of sin under which "the whole creation groans and labors with birth pangs" (Rom. 8:22). God meant that He would not destroy the earth again because of sin. This promise is a wonderful revelation of God's great grace. God issued the promise despite the fact that, even after He destroyed every living thing, the human race still retained its bent toward sin.

God acknowledged to Noah that "the imagination of man's heart is evil from his youth." And indeed, after God covenanted with Noah that "the waters shall never again become a flood to destroy all flesh" (Gen. 9:15), Noah's next recorded action was to commit sin! But God stood and still stands ready to offer pardon through grace. His grace is not known apart from sin. A spirit of repentance and of neediness is a vessel into which God desires to pour Himself in recovering grace.

That wonderful grace of God must undergird our worship. If Noah had not experienced God's grace, he would not have been able to give Him true worship. Noah's life and practice teach us a very important truth. When we attempt to live for God, to serve and worship Him, without applying His grace to our lives, our efforts result in worship that is not pleasing to God.

Having just read in Genesis 8:21 of God's awesome grace, it is easy to skip over the next verse. Here the Lord says, "While the earth remains, seedtime and harvest, cold and heat, winter and summer, and day and night shall not cease" (8:22). God promised that so long as the earth remains in existence, nature would reveal His faithfulness. To us, the cycles of day and night and of the seasons seem mundane. But it is this very cycle of nature that virtually maintains life on earth. The cycle is referred to six other times in the Bible (Ps. 33:7, 135:7; Eccl. 1:6-7; Job 26:8, 36:27-28; Is. 55:10). Even nature confirms God's faithfulness to His Word.

All of life reminds us that, although people will disappoint us, God will keep His Word. Our worship should reflect an understanding of that Word. The fickleness of human emotions is not a good foundation for worship. God is pleased instead with worship that recounts His unchanging faithfulness. Noah's worship pleased God because Noah feared God and sacrificed personal comfort in order to thank Him. God responded by confirming His grace and offering a promise of faithfulness. In our day, when worship practices are so often driven by a desire for individual comfort and convenience, we have much to learn from Noah.

THINGS TO THINK ABOUT

1. How do you think a church can strike a balance in worship, meeting people's needs without pandering to their desires?

2. How did Noah's experiences shape his attitudes toward God? Is it possible for us today to understand what Noah felt?

3. How did Noah's attitudes express themselves through his worship?

4. God was pleased with and accepted Noah's worship. How did God confirm His acceptance?

5. Can you explain in your own words the relationship between grace and worship?

THE REQUIREMENTS OF TRUE WORSHIP

Abraham's journey
    Ur - Sin (leave it)
    Haran - Growth
    · Canaan - Sin (mature -
                      handle it)

Leave Sin
Trust - not knowing details
Hear Promise & Know
        obedience = more promise

TRUE WORSHIP REQUIRES TRUST

ABRAHAM • GENESIS 12:1-8

Then the LORD appeared to Abram, and said, "To your descendants I will give this land." And there he built an altar unto the LORD, who had appeared to him.

Abel worshiped God from a righteous heart. Noah offered sacrifice willingly. So far, the evidence from Scripture suggests that worship that pleases God is an issue of the inner man, before it becomes an issue of the outward expression.

Christian leaders today are concerned with reaching as many people as possible and believe that the mode of worship is a key element in reaching the unreached. Yet any effort in effective outreach, be it religious or secular, necessarily begins with this question: Who is the audience? If our goal is to make worship more appealing and welcoming, then before addressing *how* it can be accomplished, we must determine to *whom* worship should appeal. And it is at this point that we can become guilty of what might be called *carte ante horsum*. For if true worship is based on a right relationship with God, as the Bible illustrates, then those who are not right with God cannot worship Him and should not pretend to. Adapting our worship so that it appeals to the unconverted, therefore, is a case of *carte ante horsum,* of putting the cart before the horse! As we study the Bible, we find that worship is not meant to be a practice by which a person *becomes* right with God; rather, worship is the outward expression of a heart that *is* right with God.

As we will see, the promises of God play an important role in our worship. We must know and trust in His promises so that our worship can reveal our love of and gratitude for His faithfulness. That a life-changing trust in God is a key element to true worship is illustrated by the example of Abraham. His expression of worship illustrates that a person must trust God to worship Him, and that such trust comes only from a knowledge of His Word. Here is how the story of Abraham begins:

> Now the Lord had said to Abram: "Get out of your country, from your family and from your father's house, to a land that I will show you. I will make you a great nation; I will bless you and make your name great; and you shall be a blessing. I will bless those who bless you, and I will curse him who curses you; and in you all the families of the earth shall be blessed." So Abram departed as the LORD had spoken to him, and Lot went with him. And Abram was seventy-five years old when he departed from Haran. (Gen. 12:1-4)

FAITH MEANS OBEYING GOD

God issued a clear command. He required Abraham, a man who apparently knew very little about the true God, to leave his family and home. The New Testament sheds additional light on this command. In the sermon for which Stephen was stoned he said, "The God of glory appeared to our father Abraham, when he was in Mesopotamia, before he dwelt in Haran, and said to him, 'Get out of your country, and from your relatives, and come to a land which I will show you'" (Acts 7:2-3).

We learn in Genesis 11:31 that Abraham lived in Ur before he—with his wife, Sarah, and his nephew, Lot—departed to Haran. One reason for God's demand that Abraham get out of Ur has been confirmed by archaeological evidence. Artifacts uncovered in Ur show that the city was notoriously pagan and idolatrous. Abraham, the man God chose to receive His covenants and promises, needed to separate himself as much as possible from such a sinful environment.

Notice that God told Abraham to get *himself* out of Ur. That meant that Abraham was to leave even if no one desired to go with him. In this command we see the principle that obedience to God requires us to get out of the circumstances of sin. If you or I desire to come to God and worship Him, we must first be willing to get out of sin. The true worshiper of God must leave behind all his worship of other things, for true worship presupposes the forsaking of past sinful pleasures. There is no place in true worship for the pleasing of the flesh. Just as Abraham was to leave behind the sins of Ur, we, too, must be willing to follow God, even to go alone if need be.

In order for Abraham to move out in obedience to God's command, he had to trust God. His trust would have to be complete, because God promised only to *show* Abraham the land to which He had called him. God gave no details at this point about the location of the land. Abraham had no idea where he was going. God did not even say that He would *give* the land to Abraham. Most of us today would never take a new job, much less move our families to a different country, based on such scant evidence. Any movement at all on Abraham's part required great faith. Thus the New Testament states, "By faith Abraham obeyed when he was called to go out to the place which he would receive as an inheritance. And he went out, not knowing where he was going" (Heb. 11:8).

In one way, however, Abraham's experience was not unique. Obeying most of God's commands requires trust. God has the authority to give the commands, but He does not always explain the "whys and wherefores" of the command. If God must explain all the details of His will, and then let us decide whether to accept the plan, no faith need be involved. Even if God did explain all the details, we would quickly discover that God's instructions do not always appeal to human reason. People who are "of little faith," as Jesus put it, would no doubt reject God's plan.

So God issued the command for Abraham to leave Ur, but with that command came a promise (Gen. 12:2-3). God's commands are often difficult and He does not always give a reason for those commands, but He always attaches a promise. God promised Abraham a personal blessing if he would obey. And although Abraham had no children (Gen. 11:30),

God also promised to make of Abraham a great nation. Even more, God provided for other nations to be blessed—or cursed—depending on their treatment of Abraham's descendants. Throughout human history—from the civilizations of the Canaanites and Hittites, to the empires of Babylon and Rome, and up to Hitler's Germany in modern times—nations that have set themselves against the Jews have fallen.

Yet the most important aspect of God's promise to Abraham is the ultimate promise of the Savior through whom "shall all families of the earth be blessed." Again the New Testament provides more information on this Old Testament passage. "Now to Abraham and his Seed were the promises made. He does not say, 'And to seeds,' as of many; but as of one, 'And to your Seed,' who is Christ" (Gal. 3:16). That is blessing indeed!

FAITH MEANS TRUSTING GOD

Abraham obeyed God's command to leave Ur and go to the land which God would show him. It appears that Abraham headed out of Ur quite soon after God spoke to him. Yet when Abraham arrived next in Haran, for some reason he stayed awhile. Perhaps Abraham obeyed God in stages because the command was so difficult. But eventually he obeyed God completely and left Haran for Canaan (Gen. 12:4-6). Abraham illustrated the fact that a person's obedience to God is often a matter of growth. We hear God's command but we do not understand it completely. Then we come to understand God's command but we are fearful to obey it. Finally, we learn to trust God so much that we cast away fear and do what He commands. Trust in God brings obedience to God; this truth once again brings us to the conclusion that obedience is a key to true worship.

Contrary to what human reason might expect, Abraham went where God led him only to discover that "the Canaanites were then in the land" (12:6). These people were the descendants of Ham, whom Noah had cursed (Gen. 9:25). During Abraham's time, God had dispersed the nations at Babel because of their stubborn self-centeredness. Idolatry was rampant. We read that "Abram passed through the land…as far as the terebinth tree of Moreh" (12:6), probably a reference to a place of idol worship. In other words, Abraham discovered that the people of this place despised God and loved evil.

So Canaan was no better than Ur! Why, then, did God have Abraham move? The reason is that Abraham, who was not a man of God when he lived in Ur, had learned to trust God faithfully by the time he arrived in Canaan. In Ur he was confronted with trouble because of sin, but in Canaan he was confronted with trouble because of his identification with God.

The whole scenario of Abraham's move illustrates the life of the Christian. Abraham's departure from Ur is a picture of the Christian who forsakes sin in order to become God's child. Abraham's departure from Haran is a picture of the believer who grows in faith and learns to trust God completely. And Abraham's arrival in Canaan is a picture of the Christian who must live *in* the world without being *of* the world. Faith in God marks the difference between staying in Ur and dwelling in Canaan, in the place of God's promise.

FAITH BRINGS INCREASED PROMISE

The journey of Abraham from Ur to Canaan is such a powerful illustration of faith that the story is recounted in the New Testament as an example for the Christian believer. "By faith Abraham obeyed when he was called to go out to the place which he would receive as an inheritance. And he went out, not knowing where he was going. By faith he dwelt in the land of promise, as *in* a foreign country" (Heb. 11:8-9). Yet after describing Abraham's arrival in Canaan, the Genesis account continues with a very significant development:

> Then the LORD appeared to Abram and said, "To your descendants I will give this land." And there he built an altar to the LORD, who had appeared to him. And he moved from there to the mountain east of Bethel, and he pitched his tent with Bethel on the west and Ai on the east; there he built an altar to the LORD and called on the name of the LORD. (Gen. 12:7-8)

Observe the process. When Abraham was in Ur, God commanded him to leave but also gave him a promise. The Lord told him to go to a land that He promised to *show* him. So by faith Abraham went and saw the land. Then God met with him and made another promise, a promise to *give* the land to Abraham's descendants for their possession. And at that point Abraham discovered an important fact. When he obeyed God's command, the promises started coming. Each act of obedience led to a greater outpouring of promise. His response? Abraham worshiped God!

God has given to every Christian, also, a promise of eternal possession. Those who choose to stay in Ur, to stay in their sin and reject the true God, cannot claim this promise. To them God promises only eternal destruction. Yet, sadly, even we who place our trust in Christ can get stuck, like Abraham, in Haran. We fail to make the clean break from sin. We do not grow in our faith and trust in God. Our obedience to God's commands is halfhearted, because flirtation with the world is more important to us than is the promised possession of heaven. We lose out on the ever-increasing promises of God. And if we worship at all, our worship is not true.

Abraham did what God told him to do; God met with Him and offered the greater promise; and Abraham responded with worship. He worshiped God because he believed God's promise. Abraham trusted God completely, and that trust drove him to true worship. The Bible does not say that Abraham built an altar to worship God in Ur or even in Haran. Only when he had gone in faith to the place where God wanted him to be was Abraham interested in true worship.

Notice also that Abraham continued to grow in his relationship with God. In Genesis 12:7-8 we find that Abraham actually built *two* altars. The first altar was at Shechem, the place where God met him and promised to give his descendants possession of the land. But Abraham did not stop there. He continued to move in God's will. He did not stay in Shechem but moved south to Bethel where he pitched his tent and built another altar.

Both of these actions, pitching his tent and building an altar, are significant. Although Abraham was a wealthy man who had many servants and herds, he lived in a tent. He never owned anything permanent. In the same way, if we want to be known as God's people amidst a world of sin, we must hold very lightly to the temporary things of earth. Like Abraham of old, we should instead be "wait[ing] for a city which has foundations, whose builder and maker is God" (Heb. 11:10). The New Testament uses the tent or "tabernacle," in fact, as a picture of our temporary earthly bodies, as contrasted to our promised immortality.

> For we know that if our earthly house, this tent, is destroyed, we have a building from God, a house not made with hands, eternal in the heavens. For in this we groan, earnestly desiring to be clothed with our habitation which is from heaven, if indeed, having been clothed, we shall not be found naked. For we who are in this tent groan, being burdened, not because we want to be unclothed, but further clothed, that mortality may be swallowed up by life. (2 Cor. 5:1-4)

As Christians, you and I are merely pitching our tents while we live on this earth. In addition to possessing this temporary abode, though, we should also have an altar. Just as Abraham's tent is a picture of our temporary sojourn in this world, his altar pictures our expression of worship to the God we trust.

For, when Abraham built his second altar in Bethel, he did something never before mentioned about him. He "called upon the name of the LORD." Up to this point the communication between God and Abraham had been one-sided. It all passed from God to Abraham. Of course, such is the nature of covenants: God initiates the agreement, and He sets the stipulations. Ours is not to negotiate the terms of the covenant but to accept it from God's hand of mercy and to obey it.

Nevertheless, because of God's covenant, Abraham now called upon God's name in his worship. Calling out to Him is the practice of one who trusts God's promises and agreements. True worship is not for everyone. It cannot be "adapted" for those who want to stay within their own comfort zone. True worship requires a heart of complete faith in God, faith enough to obey Him and to trust in His Word.

THINGS TO THINK ABOUT

1. Many today are concerned about reaching the lost and the unchurched. Is adapting our worship one way to accomplish this goal?

2. Why was it important for Abraham to leave Ur, making a clean break from that sinful environment?

3. List the ways that Abraham, each time he obeyed God, received increased promises. How does this pattern apply to your life?

4. In your own words, describe how the picture of Abraham living in a tent and building an altar is a picture of the Christian life.

5. What was required before Abraham could legitimately call upon God's name during his worship? What does this requirement mean today?

4

T RUE W ORSHIP A CKNOWLEDGES G OD ' S L OYALTY

E LIEZER • G ENESIS 24:1-58

And I bowed my head, and worshiped the L ORD , and blessed the
L ORD God of my master Abraham, who had led me in way of truth....

I magine moving to a new city. You want to find a church where you
can meet regularly with other Christians and worship God. Since
you have no friends or church contacts, you take out the phonebook
and start looking through the yellow pages. Under the heading
"Churches" you find dozens of advertisements. "Come worship with
us!" some exclaim, while others simply list the service times: "Morning
Worship—11 a.m., Evening Worship—6 p.m." The word "worship"
occurs frequently; in fact, almost every church advertisement in the
phonebook mentions the fact that the church members "worship."

But what does that mean?

Some advertisements highlight worship traditions that many find
comforting, from "traditional liturgy" to services that are "KJV-Only."
Others offer a welcoming atmosphere of "non-judgmental" worship, a
place where visitors can "come as you are" to enjoy caring people, and
relevant preaching and music. Perhaps most common in evangelical
circles are ads that feature a picture of the pastor, whose demeanor

and smiling face somehow convey an image that is just the right combination of "dynamic worship leader" and "regular guy."

In each case, these churches have invited you to "come worship" with them. Yet the texts of their advertisements seem to suggest that worship is a matter of observing religious tradition, or of feeling welcome, or of following a dynamic leader. Do these things compose true worship? Or have we replaced the worship of God with the worship of man—namely the worship of human traditions, of human relationships, or of man himself?

A story is told about the renowned nineteenth-century American preacher Henry Ward Beecher. Curiosity seekers would come from miles around each Sunday to hear him preach at Plymouth Church in Brooklyn, New York. One Sunday Beecher's brother Thomas spoke in his stead. When they realized that Henry Ward Beecher would not be speaking, some in the congregation got up and started for the doors. Sensing their disappointment, Thomas Beecher raised his hand for silence. "All those who came here this morning to worship Henry Ward Beecher may withdraw from the church," he announced. "All who came to worship God may remain."

How many of us are guilty of the same kind of insincere worship? We must guard against focusing on anything or anyone more than God, for God alone is the focus of true worship. When we sing, preach, give offerings, or pray during our worship, what are we thinking about? From the Bible we learn that one thought that occurs during true worship is this: God is sovereign and can do anything He pleases. Yet He sovereignly chooses to be faithful to His Word. Another example from the life of Abraham, this time describing one of his servants, illustrates how true worship must acknowledge God's sovereign loyalty.

GOD'S SERVANT FACED A CHALLENGE

By the time of the events recorded in Genesis 24, Abraham is about one hundred forty years old. And though God had promised to make of his descendants a great nation, Abraham was becoming concerned. His son Isaac was now forty-two years old and had no wife or children. Abraham did indeed have faith in God's promise.

But because he and Isaac lived among the Canaanites, Abraham was concerned that his son not take a wife from that pagan people. He realized that God's promised seed could not be pure if it came through a Canaanite woman, and so Abraham had to arrange for a wife to be brought from his own family back in Mesopotamia. Thus we read,

> So Abraham said to the oldest servant of his house, who ruled over all that he had…"[B]ut you shall go to my country and to my family, and take a wife for my son Isaac" (Gen. 24:2-4).

And so the old patriarch asked his faithful servant (probably Eliezer) to take a long journey to the east, and there to find his son a wife. But would Eliezer agree? The trip was nearly five hundred miles through solitary country with no roads or transportation services. And Eliezer, as the chief servant in Abraham's household, was next in line to be his master's heir if Isaac were to die without children. Even if Eliezer did agree outwardly, it would have been easy for him to fail in his task intentionally. He was a righteous man, however, who had always obeyed his master's will. Still, in agreeing to the journey he needed Abraham to clarify his instructions. Eliezer expressed his concerns to Abraham:

> "Perhaps the woman will not be willing to follow me to this land. Must I take your son back to the land from which you came?" But Abraham said to him, "Beware that you do not take my son back there. The LORD God…[who] swore to me, saying, 'To your descendants I give this land,' He will send His angel before you…." (Gen. 24:5-9)

Because Eliezer was a faithful servant who sought to fulfill the desires of his master, he feared that he might be unable to carry out this awesome responsibility. He was right to wonder what would happen if matters spun out of his control, as they easily could have done. He voiced concern about the prospects of failure. But his master responded with firm resolve that under no circumstances should Isaac leave the promised land. Abraham reaffirmed the fact that the whole matter of Isaac's getting a bride and producing seed revolved around

God's promise: He would give the land to Abraham's seed. Isaac could not leave the land to fulfill God's promises.

The same truth applies today. All of the details of our lives as Christians must revolve around God's promises. We cannot leave the place where God wants us to be and still expect those promises to be fulfilled. These things being true, we must make the daily decisions of our lives based on God's instructions and promises. Buying a two-dollar lottery ticket, for example, may seem like spending nothing more than pocket change. But those two dollars still belong to God. He still holds us responsible to manage them wisely. Would He want us to squander His money on a whim? But in holding us responsible to manage our money wisely, God is not asking us to do something He would not do. Abraham reminded his servant that since God had been loyal to His own promises, Eliezer should manifest that same kind of loving loyalty. We serve the same God today that Abraham served. He continues to be faithful, and so should we continue to be faithful.

Notice this truth also. The Bible does not tell us what Eliezer knew about God or what kind of relationship he maintained with God. But it is clear that Abraham's strong expression of faith helped motivate Eliezer to exercise his own faith in agreeing to perform a difficult task. Do the examples of our own lives, and the confidence with which we worship the God of our promises, similarly challenge others to trust Him?

GOD'S SERVANT PREPARED

Eliezer agreed to do his best in carrying out Abraham's wishes. "Then the servant took ten of his master's camels and departed" (Gen. 24:10). Loading ten camels for a five-hundred-mile journey was in itself no easy feat! After doing his best to prepare for the task ahead, Eliezer "arose, and went to Mesopotamia, to the city of Nahor." Nahor was Abraham's brother (22:23), so his city was the proper place for Eliezer to find a bride for Isaac from among Abraham's relatives. Abraham had even heard that Nahor had a granddaughter; the Bible reveals that after Abraham had gone to offer Isaac as a sacrifice to God, "it came to pass...that it was told Abraham, saying, 'Indeed Milcah also has borne children to your brother Nahor," (22:20). The Bible records here, too, that one of these children had "begot Rebekah" (22:23).

So in going to the city of Nahor, Eliezer was doing all that he possibly could to discern God's will. Although we do not know the exact location of this city, we do know that it was near Ur, where Abraham had once lived. So Eliezer and his entourage endured a lengthy and difficult journey. But the servant was loyal to his master and willing to take the hard road to find God's will.

How often do we as Christians want to consider the road before deciding whether to take it? Where is our loving loyalty to the God who has been loyal to us, though He is sovereign and could do as He pleases? When we find it easier to rest in Canaan and ignore God's greater desires, our attempts to worship Him will inevitably fall short. Why? Because failure to pursue God on the difficult journey causes us to miss His will and results in worship that is not true. How much of the insincere worship found in our churches today is the result of our unwillingness to trust God in the hard things?

God's Servant Prayed

The story continues. Eliezer "made his camels kneel down outside the city by a well of water at evening time, the time when women go out to draw water" (Gen. 24:11). This choice was a logical one for Eliezer in his search for God's will. Being a stranger in town, he put himself at the place where the women of the city congregated. Then he prayed and asked God to oversee the next step:

> O Lord God of my master Abraham, please give me success today....Now let it be that the young woman to whom I say, "Please let down your pitcher that I may drink," and she says, "Drink, and I will also give your camels a drink"—let her be the one You have appointed for Your servant Isaac. And by this I will know that You have shown kindness to my master. (Gen. 24:12-14)

God expects us to use wisdom and He holds us responsible to be diligent in pursuing His will. Before offering specific requests to God, our consciences should be clear. Have we really done all that we can in soul winning, or reconciliation with offended brothers, or paying our bills, or gaining victory over sin? Eliezer was doing all he possibly could to fulfill his task. Since he was looking for a young woman to be a fitting helper for his master's son, a man who happened to be a herdsman, his approach was logical. So his prayer illustrates a proper balance: he was doing everything he could, at the same time asking and trusting God to reveal more.

Notice also that in his prayer Eliezer considered God first, then his master Abraham whom he represented, and only then did he express his own petition. Even then, this servant wanted success not for himself but for Abraham. As we will see, in his humble loyalty to God and Abraham, Eliezer was able to perceive clearly God's loving loyalty toward himself. By loving others with a willing heart, we, too, can better appreciate God's love for us. When you and I willingly sacrifice our time, energy, and desires for others, we get a good view of God's kindness for the undeserving. When we serve others, we understand what God has done for us.

Since he had a clear conscience and a humble love for others, Eliezer was in a position to ask God for something that, humanly, would seem impossible. First, he expected to see a young woman show up to draw water. Second, he expected to request water and to get a positive response from her. Third, he expected the young woman to volunteer for a colossal task. Ten thirsty camels drink a lot of water! How could Eliezer have expected to succeed under these conditions? It is probable that the well was actually built like a cistern. The young woman would have had to walk down a set of stairs, fill her heavy urn, and walk back up again. She might have had to walk up and down those stairs perhaps a hundred times! No one would do that for a stranger. So why did Eliezer make this request from God? His trust in God led him to trust God more. Do our own prayers indicate that we trust God?

GOD'S SERVANT SAW HIS LOVE

Miraculously, God answered Eliezer's prayer even while he was still praying! "And it happened, before he had finished speaking, that, behold, Rebekah came out" (Gen. 24:15). She was a young woman, a virgin, and—as an added bonus—very beautiful (24:16). She agreed to give Eliezer a drink when he asked her (24:18). She even volunteered to water the ten camels (24:19-20). And she was from the right family (24:24).

At first Eliezer was dumbfounded. "And the man, wondering at her, remained silent so as to know whether the Lord had made his journey prosperous or not" (24:21). Was he dreaming? Here was a young, pure, beautiful, industrious, kind woman—watering ten camels! It must have seemed too good to be true. At last, when Eliezer learned that Rebekah was of just the right lineage to propagate God's promised seed,

> the man bowed down his head and worshiped the LORD. And he said, "Blessed be the LORD God of my master Abraham, who has not forsaken His mercy and His truth toward my master. As for me, being on the way, the LORD led me to the house of my master's brethren." (Gen. 24:26-27)

Later, Rebekah's parents consented to her betrothal. "It came to pass, when Abraham's servant heard their words, that he worshiped the LORD, bowing himself to the earth" (Gen. 24:52). Eliezer's worship expressed his sheer awe at the evidence of God's sovereign loyalty at work. Knowing that God loved and wanted to bless him, he expectantly looked forward to what God would do. These attitudes are foundational to true worship.

The same humility that Eliezer had demonstrated in his prayers to God was manifested in his worship. He realized that he was standing in the presence of the mighty God who was loving and loyal enough to intervene in man's affairs. In his worship Eliezer did not need to run, shout, jump, dance, or beat on a drum. No external action could possibly heighten the emotions that he already felt. He had just observed a phenomenal work of God, and his response was simply to bow his head and prayerfully give God glory. And he did not rejoice first for his own sake; rather he rejoiced first in God's care for Abraham.

Do we show that we care about others when we enter into the worship of God? If a primary object of our worship practices is to "get something out of it," then we have failed the test of true worship. By contrast to that attitude, Eliezer saved his own concerns for last. Having praised and thanked the Lord for His work in Abraham's behalf, the servant then expressed thanksgiving for God's work on his own behalf. It is true that Eliezer ended up in the right place because he put himself on the right path. But though he was "in the way," God led him along the way. That realization, too, is a good foundation for true worship.

Finally, let us not forget the faith of Rebekah and her parents. When Eliezer had testified to the full story of God's dealings, "Laban and Bethuel answered and said, 'The thing comes from the LORD; we cannot speak to you either bad or good. Here is Rebekah before you; take her, and go, and let her be your master's son's wife, as the LORD has spoken," (24:50-51). Rebekah, too, said, "I will go" (24:58). Although they had not experienced God's loving loyalty firsthand, they heard Eliezer's testimony and rejoiced in God's love and care. Does our own testimony reveal the sovereign loyalty of God in such a way that others rejoice in Him and are helped to choose His will?

If the proverbial visitor from Mars sat in some of our worship services today, he might conclude that we equate noise—or ritual, or tradition, or a comfortable atmosphere—with blessing. Yet Abraham's servant having seen the mighty hand of God at work merely bowed his head, humbled that He would choose to show His loving loyalty. Maybe we should long for God to humble us so that we might see the demonstrations of His loyalty to His Word. Then we can worship Him truly.

THINGS TO THINK ABOUT

1. Why is it important for you to do everything you can to fulfill God's will before going to God with your requests?

2. How can you strike a balance between doing everything you can, and trusting God to reveal more of His will?

3. Humility, as well as loving others, has a connection to prayer and perceiving God's will. Describe that connection.

4. Many people attend worship today in hopes of "getting something out of it." Is that expectation supported by Eliezer's example?

5. How did Abraham encourage the faith of Eliezer? How did Eliezer encourage the faith of Rebekah's family?

5

T R U E   W O R S H I P
S E E S   G O D ' S
F A I T H F U L N E S S

MOSES AND AARON · EXODUS 4:29-31

So the people believed; and when they heard that the LORD had visited the children of Israel and that He had looked on their affliction, then they bowed their heads and worshiped.

S pirituality is a hot topic today. Each day millions of people practice meditation to connect with the cosmos. Others search for transcendence by worshiping nature. Methods ranging from crystalline energy to guided imagery are invoked to tap the life force of the universe. Growing numbers of people practice dark arts and divination, while pop psychology provides a religion for the more secularly minded.

As Christians we sympathize with those who sense the "God-shaped void" in their lives. If only they could come to know the true God of the Bible! But then, how well do you and I know the God of the Bible? If asked to say what we know about God, many of us might reply with a statement such as "He is awesome" (describing a feeling) or "God is big enough to meet my every need" (betraying a focus on self). If these are our responses, then do we really *know* God? How are we different from the millions who equate warm feelings and self-fulfillment with spirituality? And more to our point, if our knowledge of God is lacking, then can our worship of Him ever be true?

These issues raise an even more basic question. Is it even possible to know God in the first place? The apostle Paul himself cried out, "Oh, the depth of the riches both of the wisdom and knowledge of God! How unsearchable are His judgments, and His ways past finding out!" (Rom. 11:33). Yet Paul also stated that his highest priority was that he might "know Him" (Phil. 3:10). Indeed, Jesus invited all to "learn of Me" (Matt. 11:29) and declared, "I know my sheep, and am known by my own" (John 10:14). We read, further, that "by this we know that we know Him, if we keep His commandments" (1 John 2: 3). Finally, we have this promise from the Scriptures:

> And this is eternal life, that they may know You, the only true
> God, and Jesus Christ, whom You have sent. (John 17:3)

Yes, we *can* know the God of the Bible, but *do* we? Some of us may be able to list a few of His names or attributes, even to quote a few Bible verses to prove our knowledge. But is that enough for true worship?

As late as the nineteenth century, the Bible was known throughout our culture. All educated people knew the Bible. Secular authors such as Hawthorne, Melville, Whitman, and Emerson used biblical allusions throughout their writings. This general knowledge of Scripture did not necessarily indicate a knowledge of *God*. But as compared to our times, the level of biblical literacy in those days was far higher.

Going back even further into American history, we find the Puritans. If a Puritan believer were asked what he knew about the God of the Bible, he could give a lengthy discourse on the specific attributes of God. He would be careful in his conversation to give glory and praise to God. His worship focused on the reality that God is always faithful to His Word. Knowing that Word, he knew his God in an intimate, personal, daily relationship.

Some three centuries later, the concept of such an intimate relationship is foreign to us. We do not accord the Bible the same preeminent place in our everyday lives. Yet we can take heart. God's Word recounts how His people wandered far from any kind of relationship with Him. But at last He delivered them. The experience of chastening was very humbling. But God was faithful to His Word, and this faithfulness drove His people to a true and humble worship of Him.

SEEING REQUIRES BELIEF

The greatest detective in literature, Sherlock Holmes, began his cases by knowing only that crime had been committed. He used deductive reasoning to work backward from the end result, the crime, to its original cause. In the same way, we can look at an example of worship in the Bible and then work backward to uncover how it actually happened.

> Then Moses and Aaron went and gathered together all the elders of the children of Israel. And Aaron spoke all the words which the LORD had spoken to Moses. Then he did the signs in the sight of the people. So the people believed; and when they heard that the LORD had visited the children of Israel and that He had looked on their affliction, then they bowed their heads and worshiped. (Ex. 4:29-31)

The first thing to do in investigating a biblical account of worship is to set the scene. Moses and Aaron showed up among the Hebrews, who were then captive in Egypt, bearing a message from God. It was impossible to gather all the people; at that time they numbered at least two million. So the two men called an assembly of the tribal elders, at which Aaron proceeded to reveal all that God had told his brother Moses. Then, in sight of the people, Aaron performed signs that manifested God's power. The end result was that the people believed and worshiped!

But there is a seemingly unexplained gap here. How could the people have believed the message, since that message was given only to the elders? Reasoning deductively, we can assume that the elders gave the message to the people. So when God gave mighty signs through Moses and Aaron in order to validate His message and His messengers, those signs must have clinched the people's faith. Right?

On second thought, however, the case is not so easily solved. The Hebrews had been in Egypt for four centuries. They came not through conquest but by invitation to avoid a famine in their own land. The people flourished in Egypt and were enslaved only when a new pharaoh worried that the Israelites had become "more and mightier than" his own people (Ex. 1:7-14). During this time in Egypt, the average person undoubtedly made accommodations with the dominant culture. It is possible that some had never thought about, or even been aware of the true God.

By the time Moses and Aaron appeared on the scene, the people took some convincing before they could even believe that "the LORD had visited the children of Israel." Apparently, the concept of God as a real presence in their daily lives had been lost. Even when their elders shared a direct revelation from God, the message was believed only after being confirmed by miraculous signs. Because of the people's condition, God's signs of power were necessary. They were necessary in order to arrest the people's attention.

And yet, in the end, the people did believe. How were they able to overcome four centuries of becoming progressively more distant from God? How did they arrive at a faith that resulted in true worship? That is certainly a vital question for America today!

SEEING REQUIRES UNDERSTANDING

The clues we need to answer these questions are found in the Bible. We can begin our study by doing a background check. What do we know about the history leading up to the event in question? When the Book of Exodus opens, Jacob and his sons have settled with their families in Egypt. They "came to Egypt; each man and his household came with Jacob" (Ex. 1:1), who also bore the name Israel (Gen. 32: 28). Within a generation, Israel's family was greatly multiplied.

> And Joseph died, all his brothers, and all that generation. But the children of Israel were fruitful and increased abundantly, multiplied and grew exceedingly mighty; and the land was filled with them. (Ex. 1:6-7)

Then a new administration came to power, and the trouble started. "Now there arose up a new king over Egypt, who did not know Joseph. And he said to his people, 'Look, the people of the children of Israel are more and mightier than we'" (1:8-9). Concerned lest the Israelites ally themselves with the enemies of Egypt, the king "set taskmasters over [the Israelites] to afflict them with their burdens" (1:10-11).

The Bible also records that the Israelites "built for Pharaoh supply cities, Pithom and Raamses" (1:11). These cities took a very long time to build. Yet something unexpected was happening: "the more [the Egyptians] afflicted them, the more they multiplied and grew. And [the Egyptians] were in dread of the children of Israel" (1:12). God was preserving His people in a wonderful way. So in frustration, their masters tightened the screws even more and "made the children of Israel serve with rigor" (1:13).

Further, Pharaoh ordered the Hebrew midwives to kill all male infants. But they feared God more than the king and refused to obey (1:16-17). The Lord honored their actions, "and the people multiplied, and grew very mighty" (1:20). In response to the Israelites' prosperity, "Pharaoh commanded all his people, saying, 'Every son who is born you shall cast into the river, and every daughter you shall save alive'" (1:22). As long as the king lived, the conflict between Egypt and Israel continued. But then "the king of Egypt died" (Ex. 2:23).

> Then the children of Israel groaned because of the bondage, and they cried out; and their cry came up to God because of the bondage. So God heard their groaning, and God remembered His covenant with Abraham, with Isaac, and with Jacob. And God looked upon the children of Israel, and God acknowledged them. (Ex. 2:23-25)

The Egyptian Pharaoh was cruel and forced the Hebrews to be in a bondage so painful that it caused them to groan. They were slaves. Their condition serves as an accurate picture of the person living in bondage to sin. Do you and I cry out because of our bondage? How much affliction can we take before we will cry out? The Hebrew people agonized over their bondage and cried out. And when they cried, God heard them.

Yet the words of this text do not state that the people cried out *to God,* specifically, in the same way that, for example, Abraham "called upon the name of the Lord." The Bible records merely that "they cried, and their cry came up unto God by reason of the bondage." This passage is perhaps another indication that, when Moses and Aaron arrived, the people knew very little about the true God. But the wonderful lesson is that God heard the groans of the afflicted even if their cries were not addressed to Him.

This is the context in which the people "heard that the Lord had visited the children of Israel, and that He had looked on their affliction" (Ex. 4:31). What does it mean that God had "visited" them? God's visitation, then as now, is His literal coming alongside a person in spiritual need. The Hebrew people recognized their great need. In an elementary way they understood God's presence and appreciated it. But God had acted of His own accord. He did not withhold His visitation until the Israelites had done everything right and had gotten their house in order.

Interestingly, the text records that God had *already* visited the people. They became aware of His visitation by His words, in this case His words to Moses as relayed by Aaron through the elders. The people heard the message, observed the signs confirming it, and believed what they heard. It is significant that Aaron "spoke *all* the words which the Lord had spoken unto Moses." Both men, Moses and Aaron, were careful to convey God's message faithfully as they had received it, without adding their own "spin" to the message. Even in the church today, faithful messengers must be careful about rephrasing their Master's message.

Moses and Aaron said what God said, and the people believed their message. They believed that God had sent Moses and Aaron to set them free. They believed all that God said through these messengers, even though that message was radical. Delivery from the mightiest empire on the face of the earth? How could it be? The Israelites' example teaches us that God requires His people to believe His Word by faith, even elements of His Word that are considered illogical by human standards.

"Yes," you say, "but the Hebrews also saw signs of God's power to confirm His message. We don't have these signs today!" Or do we? Today we witness the greatest miracle of all, the miracle of regeneration. When we see a changed life or an answered prayer, our attention should be arrested to the fact that there is a God who oversees our affairs.

The account in Exodus states that God's visitation occurred because He "remembered" His covenant with Abraham, Isaac, and

Jacob. Does the word "remembered" indicate that God had forgotten His promise, and that it suddenly occurred to Him that He had not been taking care of His part of that promise? Of course not! The word "remember" is a human term. God cannot forget, so He does not *need* to remember. Sometimes the Bible says that God chooses not to "remember" our forgiven sins, meaning that He chooses not to bring up those past offenses. In the case of the Exodus, the Lord "remembered" His covenant in the sense that He saw it was time to enact this part of His will. The people understood this fact. They knew He had considered their plight in His own timing and had determined to act.

SEEING RESULTS IN TRUE WORSHIP

When the people saw that God was faithful to His covenant, "then they bowed their heads and worshiped" (Ex. 4:31). Other translations of the Bible say that the people "bowed down." The original Hebrew words say literally, "They bowed themselves down." These words picture a people who were truly humbled by the reality of God's visitation. So they bowed down and worshiped, displaying a humility that was based on their newfound knowledge of God's faithfulness. Apparently these people were awed by God's action. Apparently that sense of awe is a good characteristic of worship.

In the years to follow, these very people would sometimes refuse to bow down before God. When they were determined to have their own way, God called them "stiff-necked" (in Ex. 32:9 and seven other Old Testament references). They had "made their neck stiff, that they might not hear, nor receive instruction" (Jer. 17:23). They were unbending, the opposite of being humble. At other times, the people worshiped false gods. This false worship was not characterized by humility. When the people built an idol of a golden calf, they brought offerings and then "sat down to eat and drink, and rose up to play" (Ex. 32:6). They gave license to their fleshly desires; such license is the opposite of bowing before God in humility.

The account of Israel's initial response to God's Word, that "the people believed...and bowed their heads and worshiped" (Ex. 4:31), is encouraging. But does their example apply to our own worship in the church today?

What we learn from their example is that, in order to participate in true worship, God's people must know and believe His Word. We must believe what God says about Himself and about us in His Bible. This is the foundation of true worship: to acknowledge God's perfect holiness and our own hopeless condition. You and I must trust His promise to forgive confessed sin, and then realize what a mighty work God has done in being faithful to His promise. God promises, further, to bless those who love Him:

I will guide, instruct, and teach you. (Ps. 32:8)

I will deliver and satisfy you. (Ps. 50:15, 132:15)

I will help, strengthen, and uphold you. (Is. 41:10)

I will hold your hand and comfort you. (Is. 42:6, 66:13)

I will come again and manifest myself. (John 14:3, 21)

But although it is refreshing to rehearse God's promised blessings, we must remember that the same God who promises blessing promises to punish those who sin. When we realize that His promises are a matter of eternal life and death, suddenly we understand how important it is for God's spokesmen to accurately convey His message. When preachers fail to be accurate in communicating God's requirements and promises, the result is untrue worship. What if Moses and Aaron had added to or detracted from the words God had given them? The people could not have engaged in true worship, because they would have had a false understanding of God's faithfulness to His covenants.

When we are sure that God is faithful to what He promised, our worship will reflect complete confidence in His Word. We will declare that we know God and His Word, and we will trust Him to do His work. True worship manifests an awesome respect for God. For we are astonished at His loving kindness, humbled by His condescension, and fully dependent on Him to do His will. Why? Because our God is the God of the Bible!

We would be foolish in light of that knowledge, to depend on our own strength and reason in our worship. Moses and Aaron had no thought of "adapting" worship for the needs of a people who had a low level of knowledge about God. They did not take council with the tribal elders in order to help the people "get something out of it." They merely "spoke all the words that the LORD had spoken," so that the people believed. After that, trust found its natural expression in humble worship. True worship, then, flows from a trusting heart, a heart that understands God's faithfulness to His promise.

THINGS TO THINK ABOUT

1. How can the Hebrews' bondage be likened to our own? How does God's response to their cries apply to us today?

2. Exodus 4:31 records that God "visited" the Hebrews. Does he still visit people today? If so, what does His visitation mean?

3. Moses and Aaron faithfully relayed God's words. Why was this faithfulness necessary in order for true worship to occur? Is it necessary today?

4. Worship is the expression of an attitude. When the Hebrew people believed, what attitude was reflected in their worship?

5. The attitude of the people was triggered by a realization. What did their belief cause them to realize about God?

6

TRUE WORSHIP REQUIRES SEPARATION

MOSES • EXODUS 33:1-10

*Moses took his tent, and pitched it outside the camp...[and]
every one who sought the Lord went out to the tabernacle of
meeting, which was outside the camp.*

D ancing, going to movies, listening to rock music. Preaching against these things is out of fashion today. Yet in my father's time, the theme of separation from worldly practices was trumpeted from pulpits across the land. Even in my own youth I heard frequent sermons about dress, hair length, and rock 'n roll. "What communion has light with darkness?" the preachers would remind us (2 Cor. 6:14). We were exhorted, "Come out from among them, and be ye *separate*" (2 Cor. 6:17), and, "No longer walk as the rest of the Gentiles walk" (Eph. 4:17).

On occasion, some preachers seemed to extend their view of separation to anyone who disagreed with them on even the smallest and most insignificant issues. Most preachers did not go that far. Yet as a person who grew up hearing sermons about separation, I find it strange that today there is almost an *absence* of preaching on the topic. Is separation no longer an important issue? Has the doctrine disappeared from the Bible, or have we learned to reinterpret it for today? Maybe we have discovered that it really never was a doctrine. Perhaps we grew tired of being called "negative." After all, modern society considers toleration a virtue and any form of discrimination, bigotry. How can we win people to Christ by appearing to be judgmental? Did not Jesus Himself seek out sinners?

God's people who lived more than three thousand years ago were no different from people today. God had released them from the slavery of Egyptian bondage, just as God has released people today from the bondage of sin. God gathered them to Himself, making them a distinct people, just as God gathers the Church to Himself today. But as time went by, God's people in that ancient time started to change, and their worship took on different characteristics. What were those characteristics? What caused the people to change their mode of worship? How did God feel about this change, and how did the leaders of His people feel? If they made mistakes, how can we avoid them? These questions are being asked with great urgency in the church today. Perhaps we can learn some answers from what the Bible records about the Israelites of the Exodus.

GOD EXPECTS FAITH

Three months after they left Egypt, the Israelites must still have been buzzing about their deliverance. They must have thanked God for their release and been excited to be now on their way to the Promised Land. But then God did something they did not expect. He took Moses into the hills for forty days. That act did not make sense to the people.

To make matters worse, God issued a clear but seemingly inexplicable instruction. While He met with Moses at Mount Sinai, He told the people in no uncertain terms, "Take heed to yourselves, *that* you do *not* go up to the mountain or touch its base; whoever touches the mountain shall surely be put to death" (Ex. 19:12). Boundaries would even be set up that the people were not allowed to cross! Further, God did not give the people any details about His meeting with their leader. Just exactly where did He plan to take Moses? How long would He keep him there? How would Moses' absence affect the people? God did not say, but He expected the people to trust Him.

One would think that the Hebrew people, having just been slaves in Egypt, would be accustomed to obeying without asking why. Still, in human terms, God's actions at this point seem to be counterproductive. Here was a people at a high pitch of excitement. They had just gone through the greatest moment of their lives, and now they were expected to "cool their jets" for forty days. Talk about being demoralized! Yes, the people should be able to trust a God who had done so much for them already. But since they still had a long journey ahead, why not build on the initial euphoria before it faded, and keep the people motivated for the long haul?

God's silence is our opportunity to learn to trust Him. But these people, who had seen so much evidence of God's power, chose to trust themselves.

> Now when the people saw that Moses delayed coming down from the mountain, the people gathered together to Aaron, and said to him, "Come, make us gods that shall go before us; for as for this Moses, the man who brought us up out of the land of Egypt, we do not know what has become of him." (Ex. 32:1)

In essence, they concluded, "We are unsure about God's man, so make us different gods." That conclusion seems foolish to us, as well it should. Yet are we, too, sometimes guilty of yielding to human wisdom in the matter of worship? The Hebrew people were unhappy with God's way because they did not understand Him. They thought that He must have made a mistake. Often in the church today, this kind of thinking creeps into our efforts at evangelism. We long to see more people saved, and so we get fidgety, simply too impatient to declare God's Word and then let Him do the work. But when we show disrespect to God in this area, or in any area of truth, we eventually create our own "gods." Thus in evangelism we may manipulate people to make decisions that God did not prompt. Or we may pretend that people are believers when they have not really believed. By placing human logic above the authority of God's Word, we have chosen another god.

This disregard for God's authority leads to untrue worship, even as it did in Moses' day. For as the people grew impatient or discouraged with the true God, their worship took on the traits of the local pagans.

> Then they rose early on the next day, offered burnt offerings, and brought peace offerings; and the people sat down to eat and drink, and rose up to play. (Ex. 32:6)

Interestingly, they offered sacrifices and offerings that were very similar to those that God would later require when He gave Moses the law. How strange it is to realize that these same offerings could glorify God when offered from a right heart! But in this setting, the people's worship did not glorify God; they were merely yielding to their human instincts. The word translated "play" speaks of wanton license and an abandoning of the reverence that is due the true God. The carnal ecstasy among God's people at that point was that which characterized pagan feasts. But even the pagans wondered what was going on! "The people were unrestrained, for Aaron had not restrained them, to their shame among their enemies" (Ex. 32:25).

On both sides of today's debate over contemporary worship, many Christian leaders are concerned about going too far. It is clearly possible for worship to retain some qualities found in true worship, while also taking on traits similar to pagan revelry. A congregation could in fact maintain certain traditions that point to reverent worship. They might, for example, continue to celebrate the Lord's supper, have public prayer and preaching, and take offerings from the people. But having grown impatient with God, true reverence for Him would be overshadowed by worship practices that reflect human reason or desires. The real point of attraction in these services becomes that which appeals to the worshiper. Practices that could honor God in a right setting, such as music or prayer or preaching, are corrupted. Unbelievers watch this unrestrained activity and conclude that God's people are no different from the local crowd.

GOD PRACTICES SEPARATION

God judged His people because they lost respect for Him in their worship. They experienced literal judgment when three thousand people died because of their willful sin (Ex. 32:28). Further, the Israelites experienced spiritual judgment.

And the LORD said to Moses, "Whoever has sinned against Me, I will blot him out of My book....Depart and go up from here, you and the people whom you have brought out of the land of Egypt, to the land of which I swore to Abraham, Isaac, and Jacob, saying, 'To your descendants I will give it.' And I will send My Angel before you, and I will drive out the [pagans]...for I will not go up in your midst, lest I consume you on the way, for you are a stiff-necked people." (Ex. 32:33-33:3)

God separated from the rebels. He now referred to the Israelites as "the people whom you [Moses] have brought out of the land of Egypt." God did not want to be associated with them. Rather than going with them into the promised land, God said He would send an ordinary angel to accompany them and not even the Angel of the LORD, which in the Old Testament is often a reference to the pre-incarnate Christ. The people had forfeited God's presence and power. Although He intended to keep His promise, God could not dwell in the midst of such sinful attitudes "lest [He] consume [them]."

The lesson of this account is that God separates Himself from false worship. He separated Himself then, and He will separate Himself today. When we yield to human desires in our worship, and thus detract from His glory, we forfeit God's power and presence. And when that happens, we are forced into a cycle of using human means—whether music or polished oratory or rituals or traditions—to attract the people. When we practice untrue worship, ultimately we must convince ourselves that emotional or intellectual stimuli are the same as God's power.

Nevertheless, even in the midst of inauthentic worship are those who will inherit the land of heaven because God keeps His promises. Others eventually realize that God is not a part of their worship, so they abandon their false way. The Bible records, for example, that "when the people heard this bad news, they mourned....So the children of Israel stripped themselves of their ornaments by Mount Horeb" (Ex. 33:4-6). Such mourning over sin might be genuine, or it might not be. Sometimes people mourn only because they have been discovered. Yet the people who put off their idolatrous ornaments, have been perhaps indicating that their repentance was deep and genuine.

GOD HONORS SEPARATION

What response does God expect when worship becomes untrue and governed by human methods and desires? Those engaged in such worship must, as did the children of Israel, repent and then separate from their former associations. It is also instructive to see, however, what response God expected from Moses, the people's leader. The patriarch had never engaged in wrong worship. When he saw the new practices that had become popular among the people, how did God want him to react? Should he have been encouraged by the people's spiritual striving? Should he have hoped that, by maintaining relations, he could use his influence to educate them from within?

In our age of tolerance for others, drawing lines is frowned upon. But that is what Moses did. He "took his tent, and pitched it outside the camp, far from the camp, and called it the tabernacle of meeting. And...everyone who sought the LORD went out to the tabernacle of meeting, which was outside the camp" (Ex. 33:7-9). Moses and those of like mind met with God *apart* from the people! Moses pitched his tent *outside* the camp! In so doing, he took the initiative to *separate* from the people who were not glorifying God in their worship. He was not concerned with doing what was popular. He did not even consult the tribal elders to seek human authority for his actions. His only desire was to protect God's holy name. Moses' example teaches us that, when others among God's people rob God of His due respect and reverence, we must set our tent far from the camp, apart from them.

This tent was not the tabernacle God designed and ordained; that tabernacle was not even built yet. Neither was this tent the personal abode of Moses. It was a tent set aside for a special purpose, a purpose that caused Moses to call it "the tabernacle of meeting." Other translations render the phrase best, as "the tent of the meeting." In order for Moses to meet with God, he had to separate from those who practiced untrue worship.

Moses took a stand so that "all the people rose...and watched Moses, until he had gone into the tabernacle" (Ex. 33:8). The happy result of Moses' act was that his faithful testimony brought others into a right standing with God. First, the people saw God was at Moses' tent of meeting. Whenever Moses went to the tabernacle, the cloudy pillar moved from the top of Mount Sinai to hover over the tent (Ex. 33:9). Because Moses met with God by separating from the people, the Israelites realized that God was still powerful and able to meet with His chosen people. Does our own worship give similar evidence to the people back at the camp that God is with us?

Second, Moses' separation encouraged the people to give the Lord true worship. Those who truly sought God knew they must go to the place where He would meet with them—and so they, too, went outside the camp. When Moses separated from the people to worship God, he did not go with the crowd. Yet having seen that God was with him, the people now respected his stand. This was the same Moses that the people had argued with and despised! This was the man they had considered valueless when he spent forty days in the hills with God! Now they showed respect for this man who was going to worship the God they had rejected. As Moses would pass through the camp on his way to the tabernacle, the head of each household would come to the doorway of his own tent (Ex. 33:8). At last we read that "all the people saw the pillar of cloud standing at the tabernacle door, and all the people rose and worshiped, each man in his tent door." (Ex. 33:10)

When we take a stand for reverent worship of God, those whom God is dealing with will respect our stand. Others may deride us, and some might persecute us. But those who have known the power of God's judgment and are sorry for sin will respect us. More importantly, they may be convicted of their need to worship God in truth. It was necessary for some person to stand out from the crowd and say, "This worship does not show reverence for God!" Because Moses set that kind of standard, the people back in the camp now moved in the right direction.

In our own day, worship practices are often driven by the goal of appealing to the people's desires. Are you and I willing to pitch our tents outside the camp, so that others will be encouraged toward true worship?

THINGS TO THINK ABOUT

1. When God called Moses to Mount Sinai for forty days, how did his absence contradict human wisdom? How did it lead to idolatry?

2. How can untrue worship appear to be similar in some ways to true worship?

3. How did God respond to the people's loss of reverence for Him? Does this principle apply today? If so, how?

4. When people engaged in untrue worship, what did God expect from them in order for a right relationship with Him to be restored?

5. When Moses was confronted by the people's wrongful worship, how did he respond? How does this lesson apply to you today?

TRUE WORSHIP CENTERS ON GOD'S WORD

JOSHUA • JOSHUA 8:30-35

And afterward he read all the words of the law, the blessings and the cursings, according to all that is written in the Book of the Law.

Anthropology is the study of human cultures. Suppose for a moment that an anthropologist decides to make a study of the evangelical subculture in America. To start, his study, he observes a variety of church services. Having been trained in science rather than theology, the experience is new to him. He tries to be objective in describing his observations of evangelical worship. Would his observations read something like this?

1. A committee discerns what the people want.
2. A worship service is arranged to satisfy these wants.
3. A team of musicians puts the people in a receptive mood.
4. A speaker tells the people what they want to hear.
5. The meetings attract a large following.
6. Continued stimulation maintains this following.
7. The effect of the stimulation decreases over time.
8. The process returns to the first step and is repeated.

You and I know that worship is intended to be an exercise in faith. But if we are honest with ourselves, can we not imagine how a non-religious observer might draw such conclusions about our worship? You and I might use different words. We might say that our pastor and his staff are ministering to the needs of the people. We might say that the church is helping attendees get more out of the services so that they can become better Christians or be won to Christ. But are we not forced to admit that the anthropologist's observations, although framed in non-religious terms, might have at least some grain of truth?

The evidence from the Bible so far indicates that worship of God should not be driven by human wisdom or desires. Does that principle mean that our worship should never change? In the Scriptures we can see how God set certain standards governing His people's expression of worship, and we can see how they carried out those requirements. The underlying *standards* of worship may not have changed, but, as the nation of Israel grew from one family into multiplied millions, did the *methods* of worship change? It seems logical to assume that the mode of worship for an entire nation would be different from the mode of worship within a single household, if only for practical reasons.

This question of modes of worship is as vital for Christians in our own times as it was for the nation of Israel. The church today is struggling to balance God's standards for worship with appropriate methods by which the people can express it. How can we determine, even as our culture changes with time, what are those underlying requirements that God expects us *not* to change?

WORSHIP ACCORDING TO GOD'S LAW

When Joshua began to settle God's people in the Promised Land, one of the first things he did was to draw the people together in worship of God. Since this worship centered on sacrifices and offerings, the surrounding pagans might observe the Israelites' worship and conclude that they were all doing the same kind of thing. But there was at least one major difference between the Israelites' worship and that of their pagan neighbors. After Joshua had built an altar, gathered the people, and made offerings, their worship included the reading of God's law.

> [Joshua] read all the words of the law, the blessings and the cursings, according to all that is written in the Book of the Law. There was not a word of all that Moses had commanded, which Joshua did not read before all the assembly of Israel. (Josh. 8:34-35)

Declaration of God's Word was the focus of the Israelites' worship. True worship must draw people into God's presence where they can hear, read, and study what God says about Himself, His people, and mankind in general. Those who gain in knowledge about God and about themselves through His Word will be driven to humble adoration. That humble adoration is the basis of worship, and it is impossible to achieve without an emphasis on the declaration of God's Word. True worship centers on God's Word.

Joshua led the people to a specific place, Mount Ebal, as God had commanded through Moses in the law (Josh. 8:30). There he built an altar according to specifications also set forth in the law, that the altar be constructed "of whole stones, over which no man has wielded an iron tool" (8:31). The choice of Mount Ebal was no accident. In addition to adjoining Mount Gerizim, the site formed a natural amphitheater around the town of Shechem (8:33). Furthermore, as a look at the map reveals, these two mountains were in the center of the Promised Land.

This last fact is interesting, because the Israelites had only recently entered the land. How could they march unopposed to its geographic center? Yes, they had overthrown the cities of Jericho and Ai. But did the natives yet fear the people and their God enough to let them pass? The Israelites must have wondered why Joshua was leading them to the center of the land so early in their conquest. Indeed, why had Moses commanded such a thing in the first place?

Then there was the matter of the altar. Why a plain structure of undressed stone? During this time in history, the pagans built beautiful, ornate altars for the worship of their gods. It was the age in which the use of iron tools and metalwork was expanding. Archaeologists have found evidence from this time period of bronze, gold, and silver altars that are covered with ornate carvings. How could the Israelites impress their enemies with only a plain altar of stones?

In gathering them at the center of the land, perhaps God was teaching His people to learn to trust Him for their protection. And in requiring that the altar be made of natural stones, God was making an important distinction. He did not desire for His people to make fancier or more opulent altars than the pagans made. At this point in the history of His people, God required the use of natural stones in constructing altars for His glory. Perhaps the reason God forbade tool work on the altar was to demonstrate purity. In later times, the altar in Solomon's temple would be beautifully constructed. But during the formative years of His nation, God may have desired to emphasize a distinction from the Israelites' pagan neighbors.

The principle of simplicity in worship is still in effect. "But God has chosen the foolish things of the world to put to shame the wise, and God has chosen the weak things of the world to put to shame the things which are mighty" (1 Cor. 1:27). God does not need human glitz or gimmicks to win souls. God honors Himself when we honor Him with our simple, sincere good works. Strobe lights may attract a crowd, at least for a little while. But God tells His people to, "let your light so shine before men, that they may see your good works, and glorify your Father in heaven" (Matt. 5:16).

After Joshua took the people to the appropriate place and built the proper altar, the people worshiped with offerings and sacrifices (Josh. 8: 31). Their burnt offerings illustrated thankfulness and dedication to God, while the peace offerings indicated a right relationship with God. They were thankful for the privilege of knowing God, of being His people, and of dedicating themselves to His service. They gave their freewill offerings unto the Lord, beautifully picturing the importance of offerings in worship today. In our own worship, our offerings must express obedience to God's Word and a genuine love for God. We cannot engage in true worship when we give offerings under compulsion or to receive a tax deduction. We must give unto the Lord because we love Him.

THE PEOPLE COPIED GOD'S LAW

While the people watched, Joshua "wrote on the [altar] stones a copy of the law of Moses" (Josh. 8:32). He did not personally chisel the words into the stone; that method would have taken too long and limited what he could write. The Hebrew words here indicate instead that the stones were covered with plaster. So Joshua copied exactly what God had given, which was the same law that Moses gave to the people. Joshua did not alter the law to make it more acceptable to the people who were now living in different circumstances and had different felt needs. By copying the exact law in the presence of all the people, he revealed to them that he had great respect for the law. Why did Joshua have this respect for the law? He knew that it came from God. Christians today must likewise respect God's Word simply because it is from God.

By writing God's Word in stone Joshua also pictured the importance of preserving God's principles. And the location of the altar in the very center of the land was a reminder that everyone had equal access to God's requirements and promised blessings. Similarly, when we gather for worship today, there should be no question in the mind of the people that God's Word is important. That regard for God's Word is what we need for true worship. When the excitement of the meeting is done and the "mountaintop experience" is over, what do we have left? Emotions change and fade with time, but the principles of God's Word endure forever.

THE PEOPLE HEARD GOD'S LAW

After the people saw Joshua write a copy of God's law, something very significant occurred. The Bible records that "all Israel, with their elders and judges, stood on either side of the ark before the priests, the Levites, who bore the ark of the covenant of the Lord" (Josh. 8:33).

Here we see a picture of the people gathered together, and in the very center of the crowd is the ark symbolizing God's presence. There were reminders of God's power in that ark. These included a sample of the manna that had fed the people in the wilderness, along with Aaron's rod of power and the original (second) set of stones upon which God wrote His law. On the ark was also the mercy seat where God accepted the blood atonement for sin. And at special times, God's shekinah glory would come upon the ark. All of these realities reminded the people that God's presence could be found at the ark.

The text also suggests that, in this sea of people, there was a certain order. In the center of that sea was the ark of God. Closest to it were the Levites who cared for the ark, and behind them were the elders, officers, and judges. It seems that all of the people followed the leaders' example and gathered in concentric circles around the ark of God's presence. The main point is that they were gathered around *God*. The Lord was the center of their worship. We, too, in our worship must illustrate that we are a gathering unto God. Worship should never be a gathering of the people unto a man or an organization, or unto man-made traditions or entertainments.

While the people were gathered around the ark, spreading out for many hundreds of yards between the two mountains, it appears that the leaders dispersed so "that they should bless the people of Israel" (Josh. 8:33). The passage then records that Joshua "read all the words of the law, the blessings and the cursings, according to all that is written in the Book of the Law. There was not a word of all that Moses commanded, which Joshua did not read before all the assembly of Israel" (8:34-35). Presumably, the leaders were also involved in the reading, for it would have been impossible for millions of people to hear one man speaking. This procedure was used, for example, in the time of Nehemiah (Neh. 8:1-8; see also chapter 13).

The main point, however, is that *all* the law was read to the people, both its blessings and cursings. The blessings are the positive part of the law that contains God's promises and encouraging reminders. He pledged to love and care for His people, and we still appreciate and need those promises today. The cursings, on the other hand, are sobering but important reminders that God has also promised to judge sins. We may not appreciate the warnings, but we need them as much as we need the promises. All of the people heard all of God's law—every single word! The leaders had been careful to declare the whole law. In our day, too, declaring the whole counsel of God must be the focus of our worship.

God promises that His Word is sufficient to make His people what they should be: "All scripture is given by inspiration of God, and is profitable for doctrine, for reproof, for correction, for instruction in righteousness, that the man of God may be complete, thoroughly equipped for every good work" (2 Tim. 3:16-17). Furthermore, God commands preachers to declare that Word consistently.

Preach the word! Be ready in season and out of season. Convince, rebuke, exhort, with all longsuffering and teaching. For the time will come when they will not endure sound doctrine, but according to their own desires, because they have itching ears, they will heap up for themselves teachers; and they will turn their ears away from the truth, and be turned aside to fables. (2 Tim. 4:2-4)

In the news today we hear much about "mega-churches." Having a big church is not necessarily wrong. Error occurs only when the desire is to generate large crowds rather than to trust in and declare God's Word alone.

Besides demonstrating the centrality of God's Word in worship, the Israelites' worship at Mount Ebal is interesting in another respect. The Bible records that present among the people was "the stranger as well as he who was born among them" (Josh. 8:33). Typically, the Bible does not make mention of pagans attending the worship meetings of God's people. Sometimes His people were guilty of joining with the pagans, but usually the pagans avoided gatherings where God was worshiped. In this case, however, Joshua and the leaders were conducting a worship service in which there were some attendees who might not have an affinity for God's law. Yet Joshua and the others made no "adaptation" in their worship, and the declaration of God's words remained the focus.

The same principle holds true in the New Testament. There is only one hint in the New Testament that an unbeliever might show up at a meeting of God's people. In a warning about the abuse of tongues, the apostle Paul writes,

Therefore if the whole church comes together in one place, and all speak with tongues, and there come in those who are uninformed or unbelievers, will they not say that you are out of your mind? But if all prophesy, and an unbeliever or an uninformed person comes in, he is convinced by all, he is convicted by all. And thus the secrets of his heart are revealed; and so, falling down on his face, he will worship God and report that God is truly among you. (1 Cor. 14:23-25)

In this passage, Paul writes that if an unbeliever were to come into a meeting of God's people and hear the congregation speaking in tongues, that person would conclude that Christians are fools. Therefore God's people should rather "prophesy" in their meetings. To prophesy does not mean to tell the future; the word "prophesy" here means to declare God's Word. The result of the declaration is that the unbeliever is convinced and convicted. The word translated "convinced" implies a change of heart, a change that today we might call a conversion. So in this lone New Testament reference to an unbeliever's joining God's people, that unbeliever becomes a new believer. Only then does he enter into worship with them.

From the lack of any biblical examples for attracting unbelievers through a particular mode of worship, we must conclude that the practice of arranging worship in order to attract unbelievers is not wise. The practice of enticing pagans into meetings of God's people was not popularized in America, in fact, until the mid-nineteenth century. The Scriptures reveal that God has always intended worship to be for His people. Christians in the early church met for the purpose of "continu[ing] steadfastly in the apostles' doctrine and fellowship, in the breaking of bread, and in prayers" (Acts 2:42). Their meetings were not held in order to capture new converts. They practiced true worship, making God's Word the center of their gathering. They learned what God had to say about Himself and mankind. And it was through that Word that God's people were equipped and encouraged to go out with new zeal and tell unbelievers the good news of salvation in Christ.

THINGS TO THINK ABOUT

1. Both the Israelites and the pagans made burnt offerings and peace offerings. What was the major difference in Israel's worship?

2. Why was Mount Ebal significant as the place of worship? Why a plain altar? What lessons could the people learn from all this?

3. Why did Joshua write the words of the law on the stones of the altar at Mount Ebal? What lessons do his actions illustrate?

4. What significance did the ark of the covenant play in the people's worship at Mount Ebal? What is the lesson for you?

5. The Bible rarely mentions unbelievers at meetings of God's people. What conclusions can you draw from this fact?

TRUE WORSHIP ENCOURAGES SERVICE

GIDEON • JUDGES 7:9-18

*And so it was, when Gideon heard the telling of the dream and
its interpretation, that he worshiped. He returned to the camp
of Israel, and said, "Arise, for the Lord has delivered the
camp of Midian into your hand."*

When I coached my sons' soccer teams, I taught the
boys how to dribble and pass and shoot. I explained to
them the rules of the game, the different positions on
the field, and the responsibilities of each position. We reviewed how
to execute our offense and defense. In short, as coach I tried to give
my players all the tools they needed so that, when the whistle blew on
game day, they could go out and succeed.

So, was that training all my players really needed? Of course not.
The human factor plays a vital part in a team's success as well. Many
times a less talented squad wins the game because the players are
more dedicated to team play or have a greater desire to win. As coach
I tried to motivate and encourage the boys on our team to try their
best. But at times I had to tell them, "I can show you how the game is
played, but I can't play the game for you." If the only reason they play

hard is that I told them to, why had they chosen to be on the team at all? At some point, motivation must come from within.

The same principle is true in many areas of life. When my sons began taking music lessons, for example, my wife and I had to make them practice. But the real breakthrough arrived only when the light bulb came on and our sons said to themselves, "I *want* to do this!" Then, when they were internally motivated to play music, real progress occurred.

The application of these examples to the subject of worship is obvious. The people in our churches may hear about the greatness of God and the need of men. Every Sunday they may receive good coaching from the Bible and hear pep talks from the pastor. But at some point, each team member must make up his or her own mind to go out and serve God.

In our church, I believe that my calling as pastor-teacher is to *repair* and *prepare* our people to go out and do "the work of the ministry" (Eph. 4:12). Our goal as a church is that everyone be involved in some kind of service. Is that goal realized? Human nature and individual circumstances being what they are, in any group of people—be it the church or the Rotary Club—some members are necessarily more involved than others. But among our churches today there seems to be a general feeling that unless *something* is "happening," the church must be dead or dying. So the pastor, worship leader, and those involved in planning worship services may feel the pressure to *make* something happen. They strive to elicit a response, using their creative gifts in hopes of motivating the people.

It is possible for us to be so concerned about the acts of worship, however, that we run ahead of the necessary steps God requires as He leads His people to true worship. In a sense, true worship is not an *act* but rather a natural *response* to foregoing knowledge or experience. In other words, whereas God's people can run hither and yon trying to discover genuine ways to worship God, He would rather they obediently follow Him throughout the week so that Sunday worship will be a natural expression of their relationship with Him.

This chapter is entitled "True Worship Encourages Service." But a more accurate title would be "Faithful Obedience Precedes True Worship, Which in Turn Leads to Faithful Service." Of course, that title is almost too long to fit on the page! But it does express a vital principle found in Scripture, a truth wonderfully illustrated for us in the Old Testament story of Gideon.

The main events of the story are easily summarized. God put a heavy burden on Gideon, though he lacked confidence about his ability to lead God's people. Since Gideon was weak in faith, he begged God to confirm His will by making a fleece wet or dry. God obliged and then instructed Gideon to fight a massive enemy army with only a handful of men. When Gideon was unsure, God told him to go to the enemy's camp in the middle of the night. Gideon obeyed this seemingly strange requirement and, in so doing, learned an important lesson about God's power. His natural response was to fall down in worship and then to rise and serve in confidence.

OBEDIENCE BUILDS FAITH

Gideon knew what he was supposed to do. God had given him clear instructions: "Arise, go down against the [enemy] camp, for I have delivered it into your hand" (Judges 7:9). If Gideon was afraid to scout the enemy alone, God had told him he could take his servant along. But that very night God commanded Gideon to go "down to the camp...and you shall hear what they say; and afterward your hands shall be strengthened" for the ensuing contest (7:10-11).

So the instruction was clear. But Gideon was going through a very difficult time. As the Bible records in Judges 6, many recent occurrences had brought sudden, momentous changes to his life. Because Israel was in sin, God had allowed the nation to suffer seven years of enemy occupation. All its sustenance had been destroyed, and its people were desperate. The Israelites cried out, and God sent a prophet to confirm His promises. Like all the people, Gideon, too, must have been anxious about the times in which he was living. But then God's dealings became very personal for Gideon. He was minding his own business, doing farm chores for his father, when "the Angel of the Lord appeared unto him, and said unto him, 'The Lord is with you, you mighty man of valor....Go in this might of yours, and you shall save Israel from the hand of the Midianites. Have I not sent you?'"

Gideon, however, was tentative about stepping out on faith alone. He wanted to trust God, but he struggled. So he responded to the Angel of the Lord by asking, "O my lord, if the LORD is with us, why then has all this happened to us? And where are all His miracles?" Even when God Himself reassured Gideon, still he protested: "O my LORD, how can I save Israel? Indeed my clan is the weakest in Manasseh, and I am the least in my father's house." A second time God gave assurance, but Gideon persisted, "If now I have found favor in Your sight," he said, "then show me a sign that it is You who talk with me."

God was gracious and gave Gideon a sign, followed by a promise ("Peace be with you; do not fear, you shall not die"), and a command ("Tear down the altar of Baal that your father has, and cut down the wooden image that is beside it"). He also instructed Gideon to build an altar to God and to make burnt offerings using wood from trees he was to cut down. Finally Gideon accepted God's challenge and gathered ten men to help him eradicate Baal worship in his town. But even when he obeyed the command to destroy Baal's altars, he did so at night because he was afraid. Afterward, Gideon received death threats for his action. But his father stood up for him, and, more importantly, "the Spirit of the LORD came upon Gideon." The men of his town and tribe rallied to his cause, and messengers were sent to rally other tribes.

Gideon was moving in the right direction. He obeyed God's command, then worshiped his Lord and was encouraged to start assembling an army. Yet still lacking complete faith, he "put out the fleece" so that God might give another confirming sign. God did so, and at the start of the events recorded in Judges 7, Gideon had amassed a host of twenty-two thousand soldiers. At this point in the story, however, God did an unbelievable thing with Israel's army.

> And the LORD said to Gideon, "The people who are with you are too many for Me to give the Midianites into their hands, lest Israel claim glory for itself against Me, saying, 'My own hand has saved me.'" (Judges 7:2)

God instructed Gideon to let the fainthearted go home. More than half of the army departed. Only ten thousand remained. But incredibly, God declared that "the people are still too many." So He proceeded to reduce the Israelite force to a mere three hundred men. Now Gideon had no army at all, but only a small band of soldiers. Yet that situation was precisely the place God wanted His people to be—in complete dependence on Him. Nevertheless, the whole process must have left Gideon physically and emotionally exhausted. This was his state of mind when God commanded him to go down alone to scout the enemy camp.

FAITH BUILDS ENCOURAGEMENT

Sometimes God allows His servants to reach the bottom so that they will listen more carefully to Him. There are times when God takes away everything or everyone on which His servants depend, so that they are forced to look to Him alone for help. Those are the wonderful times when God, acting out of love, makes us see how needy we really are. He is faithful to help us trust Him and Him alone.

God's instruction indicated His compassion for Gideon. Although He commanded Gideon to go down to the enemy camp, God recognized that Gideon might be afraid. "But if you are afraid to go down, go down to the camp with Purah your servant" (Judges 7:10). In practical terms, a single servant could do little against the hordes of the enemy! But having a companion was a comfort to Gideon. God's kindness to Gideon is a reminder that He knows our weaknesses. "For He knows our frame; He remembers that we are dust" (Ps. 103:14).

God encouraged Gideon, moreover, by assuring him that the scouting missions would be profitable. "You shall hear what they say; and afterward your hands shall be strengthened" (Judges 7: 11). This statement is significant, for God was not required to give Gideon a preview of His will. But because God is so gracious, He often gives us an idea of what lies ahead in the path. Indeed, in reading the Book of the Revelation we can essentially skip to the last chapter of the story and find out who wins!

Gideon obeyed, and his obedience was no small matter since "the Midianites and Amalekites all the people of the East, were lying in the valley as numerous as locusts; and their camels were without number, as the sand by the seashore in multitude" (7:12). The odds seemed overwhelming, but Gideon trusted God. To his surprise, in the enemy camp Gideon learned that his foes were apprehensive about *him!* One soldier even had a dream that, through symbols, depicted the Midianites' destruction by "the sword of Gideon," the man who had God on his side. Gideon overheard two soldiers discussing the dream.

> And so it was, when Gideon heard the telling of the dream and its interpretation, that he worshiped. He returned to the camp of Israel, and said, "Arise, for the LORD has delivered the camp of Midian into your hand." (Judges 7:15)

Like Gideon, we will not experience God's encouragement until we trust Him enough to obey Him. Often we are familiar with His wonderful promises but have not learned through experience to trust those promises. When we put God's promises to the test, however, when we find His promises are true and learn we can trust Him, then we will learn the natural joy of true worship.

Gideon certainly learned that joy! When he heard of the fear among God's enemies, he bowed in humility before his Lord. In recording that he "worshiped," the text uses a Hebrew word that speaks of a servant's or slave's lowering himself before his master. The word, frequently found in the Old Testament, reflects the Israelite concept of worship. The Old Testament worshiper acknowledged his position of servitude and dependence before his master. Thus most depictions of worship in the Old Testament show the worshiper bowing or prostrating himself in humble recognition of God. That recognition was often gained as it was with Gideon, through experience. True worship results when God allows His servants to see His mighty power and realize their own meager state.

Put yourself in Gideon's shoes. He must have been astonished to hear the enemy soldiers express their apprehension—and amazed by the way God put him in exactly the right place at the right time to overhear their conversation! Then he was humbled to realize that God would win the battle apart from his efforts and those of his meager army. Gideon could worship God truly because he had learned some important lessons from God. But in order to learn those lessons, he first had to obey God and trust Him.

In the same way, when you and I are living or acting in obedience, we learn to trust God more. As we grow in that trust, He reveals to us His great power. And in glimpsing that power, we fall prostrate before Him and worship. Does that pattern describe the kind of worship we have today?

ENCOURAGEMENT BUILDS SERVICE

After Gideon worshiped his God, he then "returned to the camp of Israel, and said, 'Arise, for the Lord has delivered the camp of Midian into your hand'" (Judges 7:15). Can this be the same man who once feared to step out in faith and serve God? Now he is striding confidently among his small band of men, rallying them to rise up against a vastly superior foe, declaring that their success is assured. Gideon is a different man! He has no doubts at all and now leads others with confidence. His example teaches us that true worship, when it is rooted in humble trust of God, encourages us to go out and serve Him.

Even more than that, true worship spurs us to encourage others, also, to serve God. Gideon's confidence was rooted in his own obedience. Before he ever challenged other servants to follow God in obedience, he first obeyed God. When Gideon threw down the challenge of obedience, he spoke from experience. He knew the blessings that come from obedience. Because he obeyed God, was encouraged by God, and worshiped God with true worship, he in turn could bring others along in obedience to God. May our own obedience and worship be so true and encouraging!

THINGS TO THINK ABOUT

1. What does it mean to say that worship is not an *act* but a *response*? What is the difference between the two concepts?

2. In Judges 6, Gideon goes through a series of life-changing events. Describe these events and what he learned from them.

3. What was the point of God's reducing Gideon's army from twenty-two thousand men to only three hundred?

4. God encouraged Gideon before his scouting mission. What put Gideon in a position to receive this encouragement?

5. Upon seeing God at work, Gideon worshiped. What qualities characterized his worship? How did he respond afterward?

T RUE W ORSHIP
R EQUIRES
C OMMITMENT

ANNAH • 1 SAMUEL 1:19-28

*I am the woman who stood by you here, praying to the LORD.
For this child I prayed, and the LORD has granted me my petition
which I asked of Him. Therefore I also have lent him to the LORD.*

When I was a boy growing up in northwest Pennsylvania, my parents would drive into town once a week to do some errands. The trips seemed a normal part of life back then. Most families had only one car, and so moms would write down their grocery lists, and then buy food for the entire week. Other errands also had to wait until then—or at least until there were enough errands to make a trip into town worthwhile.

Stores closed down at night and on Sundays, since most of them were run by local merchants who wanted to be home with their own families. Besides, who went shopping after dark? In those days, supper was a major production. Mom spent all afternoon cooking; families sat down and ate together; and cleaning up afterward was a big job. When it was all finished, we were in a mood to relax and spend the evening at home, not to go out shopping.

When my parents did go into town, they usually paid for their purchases with cash or check. Major purchases, such as a dress for mom or some hunting gear for dad, were put off until the money was saved up. It was not that credit was unknown, but you had to fill out a lengthy application and provide proof of employment.

Today, of course, we look back and wonder how our parents could have put up with so much inconvenience! Families now have two cars, sometimes one or two more for the kids. Stores are open all night, from air-conditioned shopping malls to "big box" discount chain stores. Microwavable meals and fast food restaurants mean that mom (or dad) is no longer stuck in the kitchen. Even clean-up is a snap with automatic dishwashers and disposable dinnerware. And why wait to buy a home entertainment center when we could be enjoying it now? Obtaining credit is easy! We are even "pre-approved"! In fact, we can probably get along without carrying cash at all; the checkout scanner makes using a credit card, even for everyday purchases, so much easier.

Not only do we love convenience; we have come to expect it. When we get in the slow line at the supermarket, we feel put out. On those rare occasions when "nothing is open" or the Chinese carry-out does not take our credit card, we hardly know what to do. Stoplights and traffic jams put us in a slow burn, sometimes in a rage. We buy a new computer because it can download a web page ten seconds quicker than our old one.

In our culture today, convenience really has come to be viewed as a right. If someone inconveniences you or me, we feel personally violated. How dare that person cause us inconvenience! It is no surprise, then, that today's emphasis on convenience has impacted the church. Across the country, pastors must deal with the phenomenon of "church shopping" as never before. People attend church if it is convenient. If the service is not to their liking, the following week they attend a different church.

But is such a practice worship?

True worship requires full commitment and a willingness to "stick it out," attitudes that go against the grain of today's culture. Worship may not be convenient. You might be challenged to attend church two or even three times a week. You might have to tithe on your paycheck. You might be asked to help with the church nursery or go to choir practice. You might have to miss a ball game. Perhaps one

Sunday you might not like the preaching or the choice of songs. But true worship flows from a humble heart, one that asks, "Lord, what do you want me to do?" (Acts 9:6).

THE WORSHIPER MAKES A VOW

Hannah provides an Old Testament example of someone who manifested complete commitment in her worship. As the first book of Samuel opens, Hannah is carrying a great burden. She is unable to have children. This experience is a painful one for any woman, but it was especially difficult for Jewish women who felt obligated to continue the seed of Abraham. Furthermore, a childless woman of ancient times was often left in her old age with no one to care for her. And Hannah faced individual circumstances that aggravated the problem. Her husband Elkanah had another wife, Peninnah, who had children (1 Sam. 1:2).

Should we blame Hannah for comparing herself to others? Perhaps we think Hannah should have been content, and accepted what God planned for her. (Indeed, the text confirms that "the LORD had closed her womb" for reasons of His own.) Perhaps Hannah wondered why she couldn't be like Peninnah and other women. Then again, Peninnah was not just someone Hannah ran into in the neighborhood or at the tabernacle. She was Hannah's "fellow wife." If that term sounds strange, it should. Multiple wives were never a part of God's plan. Scripture indicates that multiple wives always compete. Hannah's story illustrates the problems that arise when we step out of God's original intent.

Peninnah was not a nice person to Hannah. The Scriptures record that "her rival also provoked her severely, to make her miserable, because the LORD had closed her womb....[T]herefore she wept, and did not eat" (1:6-7). Yet Elkanah "loved her" (1:5) and tried to compensate for her barrenness by giving Hannah extra provision (1:5) and asking her, "Why is your heart grieved? Am not I better to you than ten sons?" (1:8). Of course, such prideful "reassurance" can be expected from a man who did not understand how women think. It was Elkanah who contributed to Hannah's problem in the first place when he disobeyed God and took two wives.

Nevertheless, we sympathize with Elkanah and Hannah. Who among us has never endured difficult circumstances due to our own mistakes? The story of Hannah illustrates to us how God can bring good out of our difficult circumstances by using those circumstances to draw us into greater dependence on Him. Our greater commitment to God, in turn, leads us to more true worship.

The way Hannah dealt with her problem illustrates the fact that she had learned humility and commitment. Her "heart grieved" (1:8) or, as we would say today, her heart was broken. Hannah was not merely a woman who was angry at her circumstances. Literally, the Hebrew word speaks of a heart that trembles out of uncertainty or fear. When Scripture says that Hannah "was in bitterness of soul" (1:10), it means that she was pained because of her heavy burdens. We know from our own lives that, in times of great burden, our soul is most tender and it is most ready to seek God for help. Yet it is also possible at such times to become angry with God and reject Him altogether. What did Hannah do? In the pain of her broken heart she vowed a vow to God.

> Then she made a vow and said, "O LORD of hosts, if You will indeed look on the affliction of Your maidservant and remember me, and not forget Your maidservant, but will give Your maidservant a male child, then I will give him to the LORD all the days of his life…." (1 Sam. 1:11)

Hannah willingly committed what she did not yet have to God's service. Making such a commitment may seem to be an easy thing to do, but consider the whole picture. She offered a request to God, but not just a general request. Her request was very specific: she asked for a male child. Why? Because Peninnah had boys? No, Hannah asked for a male child because she wanted to give God the specific offering of a child who could be involved in tabernacle service throughout his life.

Put yourself in Hannah's situation. What if God *did* grant her request, as she fully believed He could? She was agreeing up front to surrender the very thing she requested and wanted so badly! No selfish person would be willing to make such a vow! Only through an unselfish heart can we, like Hannah, truly display God-honoring humility. If our worship and requests are not rooted in humility, they will be rooted in selfishness.

We can envision the seriousness of Hannah's commitment in another way. Imagine a church member coming to his pastor with an unusual prayer request. The man has just entered a million-dollar sweepstakes. Now he tells the pastor that it is important to pray, because if the man wins the sweepstakes he promises to give the church ten percent. The pastor asks the man if he already tithes his income, and the man admits he does not. "Well," replies the pastor, "how can I pray for you to win the money, when you haven't submitted to God what you already have?"

By her unselfish request, Hannah demonstrated her humble submission to God. This demonstration was reinforced by her subsequent actions. "And she said, 'Let your maidservant find favor in your sight'. So the woman went her way, and ate, and her face was no longer sad" (1:18). Her vow was not an impulsive, frenzied outburst that left Hannah emotionally drained, wondering what she had promised God in the heat of the moment. Hannah was satisfied to make her commitment and trust God. This point is critical. Although her circumstances had not changed, she was satisfied to let God handle the matter as He saw fit. The next day, with a confident spirit, she and Elkanah "rose early in the morning, and worshiped before the LORD" (1:19).

Like Hannah, we too can offer God true worship when we lay everything at His feet and are satisfied to let Him do with it what He wants.

THE WORSHIPER KEEPS HER VOW

Hannah and Elkanah worshiped in the tabernacle at Shiloh, where their household had gone for the required annual sacrifice. The tabernacle was important to the Jews, for it was the place where God had ordained to meet with His people. You and I, however, have the privilege of meeting God at any time and place we choose. The book of Hebrews exhorts us to "come boldly to the throne of grace, that we may obtain mercy, and find grace to help in time of need" (Heb. 4: 16). God's presence is not represented as dwelling in a tent anymore, for He now dwells inside His people! "But you are not in the flesh, but in the Spirit, if indeed the Spirit of God dwells in you. Now if anyone does not have the Spirit of Christ, he is not His" (Rom. 8:9). What a wonderful privilege we have to bow in humble worship in the presence of the mighty God at any time!

The Scriptures record that Elkanah and Hannah worshiped at the tabernacle before returning home from the annual sacrifice. They came into the presence of God, in the manner He prescribed for them, and they bowed in humble commitment. In this case, God granted Hannah's request and personally intervened in her circumstances. Upon returning home, "Elkanah knew Hannah his wife; and the LORD remembered her" (1:19). Hannah conceived and "bore a son, and called his name Samuel, saying, 'Because I have asked him from the Lord'" (1:20).

Sometimes God gives what we ask for. At other times, God gives us something better. The apostle Paul, for example, longed to be free from a physical ailment. But God wanted him to learn about sufficient grace through weakness, and Paul was the better man for it (2 Cor. 12:7-10). But God granted Hannah's request, and she and Elkanah acknowledged His provision in the naming of their child.

By their subsequent worship, Hannah and Elkanah continued to demonstrate that they understood who was the Source of their provisions. Does our own worship indicate the same understanding? If we are self-sufficient, we will worship when it is convenient, and our worship will be cold. But if we are wholly dependent on God, we will long to worship Him whenever we have the opportunity. Hannah and Elkanah demonstrated their dependence in at least four ways.

First, they *obeyed God's Word*. They went to Shiloh each year to make the annual sacrifice (1 Sam. 1:21) because they knew God's Word required it (Deut. 12:17-18). Today, we no longer live under the stipulations of the Jewish law. But God still expects offerings from His people. Do our offerings illustrate commitment to Him?

Second, they *remembered the vow* Hannah had made (1 Sam. 1: 21). The text indicates that Elkanah agreed with Hannah's vow and gave an offering in response. Have you and I remembered our own vows to serve God? Have we honored our commitment to love and serve Him with all of our hearts?

Third, Elkanah and Hannah *affirmed the Word of God*. When Elkanah and Hannah discussed how best to honor God, they agreed that their highest priority was "only [that] the LORD establish His word" (1:23). They desired full commitment to God's Word. Do you and I share that desire? Or do we resist God and insist on having things our own way? As C.S. Lewis once wrote, "There are two kinds of people: those who say to God, 'Thy will be done,' and those to whom God says, 'All right, then, have it your way.'"

Fourth, they *returned God's provision to Him*. After Samuel was weaned, Hannah and Elkanah traveled to Shiloh where they offered up "three bulls, and one ephah of flour, and a skin of wine" (1:24). The first bull would have been used for the burnt offering, the second for the purification offering required after childbirth, and the third for the peace offering. An ephah of flour was about three times the normal offering that usually accompanied a bull. The magnitude of their offering indicated their commitment to God!

The offering of our own lives to God proves our claim of commitment, as well. We can talk about commitment, but do we prove it by giving ourselves wholly to Him? Elkanah and Hannah illustrated their commitment to God by making what, for their culture, would have been the ultimate sacrifice. For they followed through on Hannah's vow and gave their child to God's service (1:26-28). The Hebrew word translated here as "lent" means to grant upon request. How could they grant to God their only child? Could we do the same?

Clinging to what we suppose are our possessions betrays our lack of commitment to God, and lack of commitment stifles true worship. Our possessions can be tangible or intangible. We may lack enthusiasm for giving God our time or our treasure, because sacrificing those things would be inconvenient. So we keep on "playing church" and wondering why our worship lacks joy and purpose. Sacrifice may sometimes be inconvenient, but it proves our commitment. And without true commitment, there is no true worship.

THINGS TO THINK ABOUT

1. How do you know that Hannah's heart was made tender, not angry, toward God through her difficult circumstances?

2. How did Hannah's request for a son demonstrate humility and commitment before God?

3. Hannah promised to give God something she did not already possess. Was her offer sincere and credible? If so, how so?

4. The Bible states that "the Lord remembered her." God was personally involved in Hannah's life. Is this fact a comfort to you? If so, explain why.

5. How did Hannah and Elkanah, in their subsequent actions and worship, show their commitment to and dependence on God?

True Worship Requires Repentance

*"Is the child dead?" And they said, "He is dead." So David
arose from the ground...and he went into the house of the Lord,
and worshiped.*

I love to ride horses. Whether on a crisp autumn morning or a bright spring day, riding is a wonderful pastime. For me, the pleasure of riding lies in the blending of horse and rider. It can be a wondrous, almost a mystical experience. For an experienced rider, a well-trained animal becomes an extension of himself. At a light tug of the reins or the smallest pressure of the heel, the horse knows and responds instantly to its master's will.

Now and then, however, it can be fun to ride alongside someone who is new to horses. Even mounting the horse, much less riding it, is a major challenge! Once we head out together along the trail, the pace is slow. A horse knows when its rider is not in control. If the animal is accustomed to novices, it may keep going forward with little guidance. But a more spirited or independent horse will slow down, even stop or go its own way. When that happens, I often see novice riders become frustrated. Some begin shouting at or kicking the horse to make it move forward. At worst, the animal senses the rider is losing his grip on the situation.

The more the rider shouts and kicks, the less the horse responds. And the less the horse responds, the more the rider shouts and kicks.

Experienced riders know this response is a foolish one. But I have seen how foolish is a similar approach in dealing with sin. We become aware of our sin burden and resolve to repent, but we soon grow weary of the effort. So with every trial the burden becomes heavier. We respond by trying harder, but the exertion wears us out even faster. So we keep on adding to our burden until it grows too heavy to be carried. The unconverted may at this point despair of God's mercy and, with their sins unrepented of, lie down exhausted and die. As Christians, we, too, can be utterly defeated by trying to deal with sin in our own power. We may resolve to turn a new leaf, but, by leaving God out, we have failed to express true repentance, and our burden only becomes heavier.

We can respond to the sin in our lives with the same foolish attitude as that of the novice rider who kicks harder each time his horse goes slower. Then we keep adding more to our sin burden and wonder why true worship seems so elusive. We go through the prescribed motions of worship and walk away each week still unfulfilled. But without repentance—full and genuine, from a heart broken by God—we can never give Him true worship.

THE NEED FOR REPENTANCE

The story of King David's adultery with Bathsheba is recorded in 2 Samuel 11-12. David was about fifty when, contrary to custom and duty, he decided one year to stay home from the wars and let his generals lead the army. Strolling about the palace one evening, he noticed the wife of one of his generals. He conceived a lust for Bathsheba, sinned with her, and then compounded his offense by arranging the death of her husband. Not until the Lord sent His prophet Nathan, to confront David and pronounce God's coming retribution (the death of Bathsheba's child) did the king at last confess his guilt. Then David was sorry for his sin.

> David therefore pleaded with God for the child, and David fasted and went in and lay all night on the ground. So the elders of his house arose and went to him, to raise him up from the ground. But he would not, nor did he eat food with them. (2 Sam. 12:16-17)

The king fasted on behalf of the child born out of his adultery. God had declared through Nathan that "because by this deed you have given great occasion to the enemies of the LORD to blaspheme, the child also who is born to you shall surely die" (12:14). Even after a week of fasting, the infant died as God had said. The king's response amazed his servants. "Then David arose from the ground, washed and anointed himself, and changed his clothes, and he went into the house of the LORD, and worshiped" (12:20).

What happened? Why the sudden change? How could David respond in *worship* at the death of his child? The answer is found in David's writings.

David composed Psalms 32 and 51 in connection with this sin and repentance. In these two psalms, there is a clear and important six-step pattern of repentance that opened the door for David to enjoy true worship anew. It is difficult, if not impossible, for us to enjoy true worship today until we have gone through a similar process of repentance.

THE STEPS FOR REPENTANCE

The first step in repentance is *conviction*. David wrote of his unconfessed sin, "When I kept silent, my bones grew old through my groaning all the day long" (Ps. 32:3). He was miserable when he tried to conceal his sin! Furthermore, he clearly sensed God's hand of conviction, pressing down on him and drying up the vitality of his life. "For day and night Your hand was heavy upon me: my vitality was turned into the drought of summer" (32:4). Yet his awful condition was a blessing from a loving God. Fear of sin and its consequences is in fact a healthy fear. Far worse is the condition in which sin no longer bothers us. David understood that God "desires truth in the inward parts" and that, through His hand of conviction, "in the hidden part you will make me to know wisdom" (Ps. 51:6). Sin thwarts the truth, but God-sent conviction brings wisdom.

Confession of sin is the second step in true repentance. "I acknowledged my sin to you," wrote David, "and my iniquity I have not hidden" (Ps. 32:5). Note that David confessed even though he realized that God already knew about his sin. By ending the cover-up, David was bringing himself into agreement with God. The same agreement is expressed in Psalm 51:3-4: "For I acknowledge my transgressions: and my sin is always before me. Against You, You only, have I sinned, and done this evil in Your sight." Although it is true that he had hurt others, David keenly felt that his transgression was first against God. Confession to God, therefore, is required for true repentance to occur.

Confession is insincere unless there is a genuine *desire* to agree with God about the sin. That desire is the third step. David recorded that "I said, I will confess my transgressions to the LORD" (Ps. 32: 5). He did not argue with God or put forth an excuse. He recognized that God had every right to "hide [His] face from my sins" (51:9) and that it was His prerogative to "have mercy upon me" (51:1a). Asking for mercy was recognition that it is God alone who helps the helpless. David longed to be forgiven (51:1b), cleansed (51:2), and healed (51:8) by God. He yearned for restored fellowship with Him (51:7-12) and to be delivered from his guilt and depression (51:14). He acknowledged that God had broken him (51:8). This work was necessary, however, before the Lord could "create in [him] a clean heart" and "renew a steadfast spirit within [him]" (51:10). Clearly, David desired to be in agreement with God!

Such agreement brings *assurance*. After all, agreeing with God necessarily means knowing that He really can do what He says He can do. "Purge me...and I shall be clean; wash me, and I shall be whiter than snow" (Ps. 51:7). David was sure that happiness comes from knowing that, for those who sincerely repent, God forgives sin and gives righteousness in its place. "Blessed is he whose transgression is forgiven, whose sin is covered. Blessed is the man to whom the Lord does not impute iniquity, and in whose spirit there is no deceit" (Ps. 32:1-2). Beyond simply stating a general principle, David declared his assurance that God had acted in his own case, that He "forgave the iniquity of [his] sin" (32:5). David was secure in the knowledge that God was his "hiding place; You shall preserve me from trouble" (32:7). Only a forgiven sinner can hide *in* God, for the unrepentant seeks instead to hide *from* God!

The fifth step for the repentant sinner is *commitment*. "For this cause [the cause of forgiveness] everyone who is godly shall pray to You in a time when You may be found" (32:6). Godly people actively respond to God's chastening. David's response included not only prayer, but also sharing what he had learned with others. "I will instruct you and teach you in the way you should go" (32:8), he declared, resolving to "teach transgressors Your ways. He affirmed that "then sinners shall be converted to You" (51:13). Like David, the penitent sinner is committed to being used by God for His glory.

Worship is the sixth and final step in the process of repentance described by King David. The forgiven sinner revels in the fact that God "shall surround me with songs of deliverance" (32:7). Those whose transgressions have been covered declare with David, "Be glad in the Lord, and rejoice, you righteous: and shout for joy, all you upright in heart" (32:11). The king did, in fact, conclude the process of repentance by offering acceptable sacrifices to God (51:19). But true repentance is not expressed by simply going through the motions of worship. A broken and contrite sinner expresses himself in worship that comes from the heart.

> O Lord, open my lips, and my mouth shall show forth Your praise. For You do not desire sacrifice, or else I would give it; You do not delight in burnt offering. The sacrifices of God are a broken spirit, a broken and a contrite heart—these, O God, You will not despise. (Ps. 51:15-17)

Notice that David's worship was the result of God's opening his lips. His songs and praises of worship came from submission to and communion with God—and that communion resulted from a repentant heart. Jesus Himself, when He ordained our observance of the Lord's Supper, commanded that prior to worship "a man [should] examine himself, and so…eat of the bread, and drink of the cup" (1 Cor. 11:28). Apart from God's breaking our hearts in repentance from sin, the religious traditions that we call "worship" fail the test of true worship. Would that we would remember the words of the prophet Samuel:

> Has the LORD as great delight in burnt offerings and sacrifices, as in obeying the voice of the LORD? Behold, to obey is better than sacrifice, and to heed than the fat of rams. (1 Sam. 15:22)

THINGS TO THINK ABOUT

1. *Conviction* is the first step in repentance as described by David. Has God ever convicted you about a sin? How did you know you were experiencing conviction?

2. *Confession* is the second step. Why must you confess a sin, not only to those you have hurt, but first to God?

3. *Desire* to be in agreement with God about a sin is the third step. How did you express this desire after an occasion when you sinned?

4. *Assurance* is the fourth step. When you have confessed a sin to God, how do you know for sure He has forgiven you?

5. *Commitment* is the fifth step. How did you respond when God forgave you? How did this response show commitment to Him?

11

TRUE WORSHIP REQUIRES INTEGRITY

JEROBOAM • 1 KINGS 12:25-33

Therefore the king asked advice, made two calves of gold, and said to the people, "It is too much for you to go up to Jerusalem."

Many years ago, my father was considering the purchase of a small van. In those days, such vehicles were often lightweight and tended to be blown around by the wind. Dad asked the salesman about this problem, and the fellow assured him that such concerns were baseless rumors. My father bought the van and, for the next few years, experienced the excitement of being blown across the interstate by the wind and by passing eighteen-wheelers. Some time later, Dad was visiting another local dealer when he encountered the same salesman, now selling a different brand of vehicle. The man did not recognize my father, so Dad led the conversation around to camper vans. When Dad said that they tend to be blown around by the wind, the salesman enthusiastically agreed!

Whether fairly or not, we have come to expect a lack of integrity in used car salesmen. Sadly, the same flaw can be found all too often among the clergy. In fact, a lack of integrity in motives is a common theme in religious history and is frequently described in the Bible. A religious leader may begin with pure motives. But when things get tough, he abandons trust in God and relies on his human wisdom. To worship God in name, but to rely on yourself in fact, is to lack integrity.

The Old Testament king Jeroboam teaches us, through his unfortunate failure, a very important lesson about integrity of motives in worship.

THE STORY EXPLAINED

When Solomon was still king over a united Israel, he regarded Jeroboam as a brave and hard-working man, and entrusted him with great administrative responsibility. As recorded in 1 Kings 11, God then sent to Jeroboam a prophet who revealed that God would divide the kingdom because of the people's idolatry. Jeroboam was to be king over ten of the nation's twelve tribes. Solomon attempted to have Jeroboam assassinated, but he fled in exile to Egypt.

We read in 1 Kings 12 that when Solomon died and his son Rehoboam became king, Jeroboam returned from exile. Because Solomon had imposed oppressive taxation, the people asked their new ruler for relief. Rehoboam responded with the promise of even greater oppression, and the people rebelled and killed his tax collector. Having heard that Jeroboam was returned from exile, the people made this former administrator their king. Rehoboam meanwhile fled from Shechem to Jerusalem, gathered the two southern tribes about him, and prepared to launch a civil war. But God intervened by sending His prophet to tell Rehoboam and his followers not to fight.

God also made promises to Jeroboam, affirming that He Himself was the cause of the events that were to come. It was *God* who would divide the kingdom, *God* who would "give" ten of the tribes to Jeroboam, and *God* who would "make" him king. Not shrewd political maneuvering, but rather the call of God, would gain Jeroboam his throne. God made Jeroboam a further promise:

> Then it shall be, if you heed all that I command you, walk in My ways, and do what is right in My sight, to keep My statutes and My commandments, as My servant David did, then I will be with you and build for you an enduring house, as I built for David, and will give Israel to you. (1 Kings 11:38)

Because of this marvelous call from God and because of His promises, Jeroboam quickly undertook the task of building or fortifying key cities. But perhaps a politician at heart, Jeroboam began to fear for his position. What would happen if the tribes he ruled, which lived in the north, traveled south to Jerusalem for their traditional worship? "If these people go up to offer sacrifices in the house of the LORD at Jerusalem, then the heart of this people will turn back to their lord, Rehoboam king of Judah, and they will kill me and go back to Rehoboam king of Judah" (1 Kings 12:27).

Rather than trusting God's promises, Jeroboam reacted to his fears with a plan of his own devising. To keep his people from going to Jerusalem, Jeroboam created a new religion whose seat was in the north. True worship of God was replaced by a man-made system. Ironically, Jeroboam ignored the fact that idolatry was the reason that God divided the nation and made him a king in the first place!

Jeroboam made two golden calves, a practice he likely learned during his exile in Egypt. The sight of the calves would not have shocked his subjects, for such supplements to worship were common among their pagan neighbors. Most pagans did not consider the calves themselves to be gods; they simply considered them to mark the place where the gods stood. Jeroboam probably did not want his people to worship the calves but to worship Yahweh, who now stood, supposedly, on the backs of the calves. In essence, Jeroboam was attempting to move God's presence from the ark in Jerusalem to the calves in the north.

This was a more convenient arrangement, Jeroboam told the people, for "it is too much for you to go up to Jerusalem" (1 Kings 12: 28). He even put a spiritual spin on his move, claiming that the calves were a reminder of how God had brought the nation out of Egypt! Jeroboam had forgotten the lesson of Mount Sinai, where the nation worshiped the golden calf of Aaron and three thousand people died.

In his human wisdom, the king placed shrines in Bethel and Dan. Since Bethel was on the southern border of Judah, his subjects who were heading south had an excuse not to go to Jerusalem. And since Dan was the northernmost city in his kingdom, Jeroboam had all his geographic bases covered.

In time, Jeroboam established a counterfeit method of worship. He built houses of worship similar to the temple in Jerusalem — though much smaller and far less ornate — but also similar to pagan shrines. Thus the people could be like their neighbors while enjoying a semblance of their own tradition. The Bible records that Jews who lived far from Jerusalem often fell into such false worship. The king further pandered to popular appeal by appointing "priests from every class of people, who were not of the sons of Levi" (12:31). This practice was contrary to the law (Deut. 10:8, 21:5); but Jeroboam found it more convenient and popular to appoint people who were not qualified by God's standard. To compound the problem, the king's rejection of the true Levites prompted them to leave his kingdom altogether and emigrate to the south (2 Chron. 11:14).

Jeroboam also counterfeited true worship when he instituted feasts similar to those God ordained. Jeroboam's feast was scheduled to take place about one month after the Feast of Tabernacles. That was one of the chief feasts in the Jewish calendar and one that God required His people to attend in Jerusalem (Deut. 16:16). Jeroboam gave the people an alternative so that they would not feel obligated to worship in the way that God prescribed. Jeroboam's feast, with its sacrifices burning on the altar, even looked much like God's prescribed feast.

All of this, as the Scriptures record in a significant statement, was a scheme "which [Jeroboam] had devised of his own heart" (1 Kings 12:33). The worship appeared to be much like God-ordained worship, but it was in reality the creation of a man who did not trust God. He created a false form of worship in order to protect his personal interests. We look at Jeroboam and wonder how someone could be so lacking in integrity. Yet his failure is repeated today with regularity!

THE STORY APPLIED

The example of Jeroboam teaches us that failure to trust God results in self-reliance. God is still the sole authority who has the right to call people to do His work. This truth is clearly stated in the New Testament.

> And He Himself gave some to be apostles, some prophets, some evangelists, and some pastors and teachers, for the equipping of the saints for the work of ministry, for the edifying of the body of Christ. (Eph. 4:11-12)

This passage of Scripture lays the foundation for God's work in the Church. God *calls* His workers and *gives* them gifts to do His work. That work is to equip the saints—to repair spiritual problems common among believers—and to prepare them for service. When the saints do "the work of ministry," the body of Christ is strengthened and ongoing spiritual growth results (Eph. 4:13-16). If God did not call the servant, therefore, that servant is an imposter who is drawing on human wisdom, and he will not edify the body of Christ. On the other hand, a God-called leader has God's promise of success if he obeys the Word of the One who called him.

Nevertheless, God-called leaders must continue to trust Him. Since every church faces difficulties, exercising trust is not an easy task. As a pastor, I constantly have questions about the best method for inspiring worship among God's people. I want the people whom God has placed under my responsibility to know Him better and be drawn into closer fellowship with Him. Those goals require a method for accomplishment, if only because the church is made up of imperfect people. But when results seem to be lacking, a pastor may start to doubt his methodology. Why does the church down the road always seem to attract more people? Why is the preacher on the other side of town getting more attention? Even a God-called leader may fall into the trap of modeling his methods upon what "successful" pastors are doing.

The failure of Jeroboam teaches us two important principles. First, we learn that we dare not cease to trust the God who called us to our task and turn instead to human wisdom. Second, we learn that trust in self rather than in God produces a lack of integrity in worship. We may create a type of worship that looks very much like God-prescribed worship. We may continue to follow certain traditions (meeting in a church building, using music and preaching) while creating worship that appeals to what is popular. But such worship is popular to whom? The task of a God-called leader is to equip *believers* to do the work of the ministry. Worship is therefore not a tool whereby church members can bring in people to *become* saved. True worship instead encourages believers to go out and win the lost, then bring people to church once they *are* saved.

That concept alone destroys any need to be like Jeroboam creating worship practices that appeal to the masses. Indeed, relying on human wisdom, catering to what is popular, actually causes people to sin. If our goal in worship is increased appeal, we must necessarily "adapt" our worship, with the result that we hide God. After all, His holiness is offensive to those who harbor sin. But by making the gospel of no offense, we really make the gospel of no effect. Pretending to draw people *to* God, we ultimately drive people *from* Him!

Am I suggesting that pastors and churches should not be concerned about poor facilities or poor programming? Of course not. But the first order of business is for us to trust the truth of God's Word enough to proclaim it with full integrity. Human wisdom may attract a crowd, at least for a time. But the root of true worship, aptly described by the apostle John, is this:

> That which we have seen and heard we declare to you, that you also may have fellowship with us; and truly our fellowship is with the Father and with His Son Jesus Christ. And these things we write to you that your joy may be full. (1 John 1:3-4)

Things to Think About

1. What caused Jeroboam to cease trusting God and rely on his own wisdom? Can this pattern still occur in the church today?

2. List the ways Jeroboam created man-made worship. How did it resemble God-ordained worship? How does the example of Jeroboam's worship apply today?

3. God calls leaders to "equip the saints." What can happen if this leader is not called? or if he is called, he ceases to trust God?

4. Explain in your own words why reliance on human wisdom, rather than on God, produces a lack of integrity in worship.

5. Jeroboam created a system of worship designed to be popular. Why is it that this approach actually drives people *away* from God?

PART 2

THE MARKS OF TRUE WORSHIP

12

TRUE WORSHIP STARTS WITH A PROPER ATTITUDE

DAVID • 1 CHRONICLES 16:1-7 • PSALM 96

*On that day David first delivered this psalm into the hand of
Asaph and his brethren, to thank the Lord.*

Worship should be exciting. But what exactly does
excitement in worship involve? The Super Bowl is
exciting, yet somehow we know that worship should
not be exciting in the same way. How do we explain the difference?

As a child I got excited about Christmas morning. As a young
man I got excited about my graduation day and wedding day. Then
I got excited when my first child was born; and now in middle age I
was excited again to stand as best man at my son's wedding. Each of
the events was exciting, but each was exciting in a different way. My
childhood excitement at Christmas centered on my desires. When I
grew older and progressed through my graduation and my wedding,
then the births of my sons, my excitement came from a different
source. Though I could not yet understand their full significance, I
was awed and sobered by events that were bigger than myself. Years

later, as my eldest son took a wife, my excitement stemmed from a glad appreciation of everything that had led up to that day.

Is this distinction the best way to understand the difference between the excitement of a Super Bowl and the excitement of true worship? Certainly, worship goes beyond self and involves a trusting awe over what God *will* do and a mature appreciation for what He *has* done. Our study so far confirms these facts. But these truths speak of soberness and humility. What about *excitement*? King David, for example, is portrayed in the Bible as dancing and singing and giving praises to God. He was obviously excited in his worship! Does exciting worship consist merely of such obvious demonstrations? In learning what the Bible has to teach us about worship, the example of King David is instructive.

TWO EXAMPLES OF EXCITEMENT

The cause of the king's excitement, the event that made him dance and sing, was the coming of the ark of the covenant to Jerusalem. More than twenty years earlier, the Philistines had taken the ark when they defeated Israel in battle (1 Sam. 4:11). But the pagans thereby brought calamity on themselves, and, so after seven months they returned the ark to Israel along with a tribute of gold. The Philistines simply put the ark and the gold offering on a cart, tied two oxen to the cart, and then abandoned it. Wheat farmers in a border district discovered the ark. When these men violated the ark, God struck down possibly more than fifty thousand of their number.

Chastened, the people sent the ark to the border city of Kirjath-jearim. But the tragedy of the citizens' death had a salutary effect. Over the next twenty years that the ark remained in Kirjath-jearim, "all the house of Israel lamented after the LORD" (1 Sam. 7:2). Their hearts made tender, the people now hearkened to God's words through the prophet Samuel. Revival swept the land and, as God promised, Israel won a great victory, defeating the Philistines once and for all.

After David became king, he decided that the ark should be brought to Jerusalem and placed in a tabernacle that he was having built. A grand procession was planned: the ark was placed on a cart and accompanied by

"David and all the house of Israel [who] played music before the Lord on all kinds of instruments" (2 Sam 6:5). The people engaged in rejoicing, music, and praise. It was a very exciting moment!

But as events proved, the worship of the people was not true. They failed to acknowledge God's holiness. They treated the ark, which God called sacred, as if it were just another piece of religious furniture. For one thing, they transported the ark using a cart which was not the means prescribed by God for transporting the ark (Ex. 25: 14). Then, when the cart teetered under the pull of the oxen, one of the attendants put his hand on the sacred ark to steady it. So disrespectful was the man's action that "God struck him there for his error; and he died there by the ark of God" (2 Sam. 6:7). The procession made it only as far as Obed-Edom. There the ark stayed.

Three months later, David finished building the tabernacle that would house the ark. He decided to make a second attempt at bringing the ark to Jerusalem. Once more, the grand event was accompanied by much joy and singing.

> [W]hen those bearing the ark of the LORD had gone six paces, that he sacrificed oxen and fatted sheep. Then David danced before the LORD with all his might; and…Israel brought up the ark of the Lord with shouting and with the sound of the trumpet. Now as the ark of the LORD came into the City of David…King David [was] leaping and whirling before the LORD. (2 Sam. 6:13-16)

The king and his people were obviously excited! But something about their worship was different this time. This time David had obeyed God's instruction. Notice that the ark was now borne by porters in the manner God had prescribed. A proper recognition of God's holiness was also demonstrated by starting the procession with a sacrifice. When the ark arrived in Jerusalem, "they brought the ark of God, and set it in the midst of the tabernacle that David had erected for it. Then they offered burnt offerings and peace offerings before God" (1 Chron. 16: 1). The worship was suffused with great solemnity, but also with great excitement. David appointed priests to play harps, psalteries, cymbals, and trumpets "regularly before the ark of the covenant of God" (16:6). Even the king himself composed a song especially for the occasion.

Which is the lesson in this example? We have seen two instances of worship, both of which involved great excitement. Both featured music, singing, and rejoicing. But one ended in disaster—worship cut short, a man dead, and God angry. The other expression of worship was successfully concluded, and the people were blessed. Both expressions were exciting but in only one instance did God accept the worship. What was the difference?

The difference was the *attitude* in which the worship was offered. We have already seen how, in the first attempt to transport the ark, God was disobeyed and His presence—symbolized in the ark—was carelessly regarded. But in the second attempt God was obeyed, and, through offerings and praises, His person was the focus of His people's worship.

The attitude that made the difference can be seen in the song that David composed upon the ark's return. The Bible records what was in the heart of God's man as he participated in worship that was both exciting *and* true. David's song, recorded in 1 Chronicles 16:8-36, is actually a compilation of three psalms David had written, apparently, on earlier occasions. The middle section of David's song was based on what is now preserved in the Bible as Psalm 96. In this psalm we find the theme of the entire song, expressing the essence of true, joyful worship. "Oh, worship the LORD in the beauty of holiness! Tremble before Him, all the earth" (Ps. 96:9).

THE PROPER ATTITUDE FOR WORSHIP

In this song David issues a call to worship, a worship that is joyful and fearful at the same time. Can this kind of worship really take place? How do we resolve this seeming contradiction of attitudes?

Fear stems from the fact that, when we say God is holy, we acknowledge His complete separation from sin. He avoids contact with sin and is offended by our sins. God's holiness leaves you and me in a difficult situation. To resolve this difficulty, some suggest that the Church today should not focus on God's holiness; that focus might turn people away from God's love. But David resolved the difficulty by describing God's holiness as "beautiful."

Why beautiful? The person who loves sin knows in his conscience that he offends God, and so he regards God's holiness as austere and restrictive. But that same holiness is beautiful to the person whom God has delivered from sin's power and penalty. The repentant sinner trembles at the thought of his position before a holy God, but he rejoices in the truth that only a God who is perfectly sinless could have the power to save him.

David's call to worship is first of all, therefore, a call to fear. For if we see the holy God as all that He is, we will fear greatly. Fearing God is the first step. The second step occurs when our fear matures into awesome respect for the beauty of His holiness. Such maturation takes place when we understand God's love and forgiveness more fully. In the third step, as our understanding of God increases, two things will happen. We will fear all the more at the thought of offending Him who loves us. But we will rejoice all the more as we contemplate the consummation of His deliverance.

> Let the heavens rejoice, and let the earth be glad; let the sea roar, and all its fullness; let the field be joyful, and all that is in it. Then all the trees of the woods will rejoice before the LORD. For He is coming, for He is coming to judge the earth. He shall judge the world with righteousness, and the peoples with His truth. (Ps. 96:11-13)

In the New Testament we learn that "the whole creation groans and labors with birth pains together until now. Not only that, but we also who have the firstfruits of the Spirit, even we ourselves groan within ourselves, eagerly waiting for the adoption, the redemption of our body." (Rom. 8:22-23). If the literal earth groans under the curse of sin and rejoices at the thought of the Creator's coming, we who likewise groan should also rejoice as we look forward to the day of full redemption. Our hedonistic culture finds it hard to combine reverence and joy. Yet the very combination of joyful reverence and expectation should infuse our worship with excitement! How can our worship possibly be dreary?

THE PROPER ACTIONS FOR WORSHIP

David's song before the ark of the covenant teaches that a proper *attitude* in worship will be manifested in proper *actions* in worship. Specifically, David describes three categories of actions: singing, proclaiming, and offering.

He who worships truly must *sing* a new song unto the holy God. "Oh sing to the LORD a new song! Sing to the LORD, all the earth. Sing to the LORD, bless his name" (Ps. 96:1-2a). A new song is a fresh song, a song that is different from the old kind of song that illustrates the effects of sin. The new song that God deserves is a song that blesses His name. It is a song that is directed to Him and that exalts His character, which is rooted in His name.

A proper attitude in worship will be manifested in our *proclamations*. "Proclaim the good news of His salvation from day to day. Declare His glory among the nations, His wonders among all peoples....Say among the nations 'The LORD reigns'" (96:2-3,10). True worship proclaims the inexhaustible good news of God's salvation every day. Encouraged by the message of salvation as we worship in God's house, we will take that message out "among the heathen" who need to hear of His glory, His wonders, and His reign.

Finally, a proper attitude of joyful reverence in worship will express itself in acceptable *offerings*. "Give to the LORD, O families of the people, give to the LORD glory and strength. Give to the Lord the glory due His name; bring an offering, and come into His courts" (96:7-8). Words of praise are important in giving God the glory due His name. But all too often our words are cheap! True words of praise to God, in contrast, are backed by sacrifice. Can you and I honestly praise God, with a proper attitude of fear, when all the while we are robbing Him? The Lord addresses this matter in the book of Malachi: "Will a man rob God? Yet you have robbed me. But you say, 'In what way have we robbed you?' In tithes and offerings" (Mal. 3:8).

THE PROPER ANCHOR FOR WORSHIP

True worship starts with a proper *attitude* that manifests itself in proper *actions*. But in the final analysis, worship does not begin with us at all; it finds its proper *anchor* in the worthiness of God. The English word "worship", in fact, is derived from the phrase "worth ship." To state the concept simply, we must offer true worship to God because He is worthy.

> For the LORD is great and greatly to be praised; He is to be feared above all gods. For all the gods of the peoples are idols, but the LORD made the heavens. Honor and majesty are before Him; strength and beauty are in His sanctuary. (Ps. 96:4-6)

God's worth is revealed in His greatness and supremacy, honor and majesty, strength and beauty. Some people stop at this point: they contemplate God's worthiness and express their admiration. Their worship might include some excitement, just as did the worship of the people of Israel the first time they attempted to bring the ark into Jerusalem. But a proper excitement in worship occurred only when the people obeyed God. Their obedience was rooted in a proper fear of and reverence for Him.

As David reminded his hearers—and as his psalm teaches us today—the God of majesty and beauty is also the God who "is coming to judge the earth. He shall judge the world with righteousness, and the peoples with His truth" (96:13). There is coming a final day when God will make an end of this world. Then will "the dead, small and great, stand before God." Observing the scene, John records that "the books were opened. And anyone not found written in the book of life was cast into the lake of fire" (Rev. 20:12,15).

God's judgment will not depend on what you or I think. No human opinions will matter on the day of judgment. People who have worshiped idols of their own making—whether those idols are power, pleasure, or position—will be humbled before the only true God. True worship must express praise to the God who is described in this Bible. Do you know that God? Does your worship indicate, by your attitude and action, that you know the God who is defined in His Word?

THINGS TO THINK ABOUT

1. Explain in your own words the differences between the first and second attempt to bring the ark to Jerusalem.

2. How can joy and fear coexist in worship? Why must fear precede joy, and why is it that joy is not possible without fear?

3. Fear of God is the beginning of true worship. But how does that fear mature? Once matured, how is it expressed?

4. A proper attitude in worship shows itself in three proper actions. List them, and then describe how they apply to your situation.

5. Why is it wrong for worship to stop with praising God for His majesty? What important aspect of God's nature would such worship omit?

TRUE WORSHIP STARTS WITH A PROPER UNDERSTANDING

NEHEMIAH • NEHEMIAH 8:1-8

So they read distinctly from the book, in the Law of God; and they gave the sense, and helped them to understand the reading.

When God began His Church, the new believers met together and "continued steadfastly in the apostles' doctrine and fellowship, and in the breaking of bread, and in prayers" (Acts 2:42). Of the four activities—learning doctrine, having fellowship, breaking bread, and praying to God—which do you think was the most important?

Fellowship was certainly necessary for the encouragement of a small and persecuted band of believers. Breaking bread in remembrance of Christ's atoning death served to keep their cause in focus. Prayer was essential as the believers faced the tremendous social and legal pressures arrayed against them. Compared to these elements of worship, learning "dry" doctrine must have seemed almost of secondary importance.

Or did it? Today, an emphasis on doctrine is often viewed as unloving, divisive, or legalistic. Yet for those first Christians, learning from the apostles the teachings of Jesus was the most important activity of all. Without these teachings, they would not have understood how or why to pray. They would not have understood the need for fellowship, or even what the breaking of bread signified. The teaching and preaching of God's Word, therefore, was a critical aspect of worship in the early Church.

In the centuries that followed, the early church era, professional clerics came to preside over church worship. Later, these clerics found they could enhance their power by keeping the people ignorant of the Bible. As the self-proclaimed final arbiters of God on earth, they could wield great temporal as well as religious power. They conducted worship in languages that were foreign to the people. And these church leaders prevented the people from having God's Word in their native tongues. Anyone who sought after truth was compelled to accept the word of the clergy. Although it is probable that a far higher percentage attended church services than is common today, millions lived and died without ever knowing the Christ of the Scriptures.

The reformers made many attempts to make God's Word available to the people. For centuries, these efforts were thwarted by the clerical system. But at last its power waned sufficiently, and the reformers were able to establish churches of their own. Bibles were printed in the languages of the people, and the teaching of God's Word again became a vital aspect of worship.

But the growing secularization, which had conquered the power of the clerics, carried with it the seeds for a new age of biblical ignorance. More than a century ago, scholars and skeptics began to question whether the Bible was truly the Word of God. Because their appeal to human wisdom was in tune with the spirit of the age, the world was soon persuaded to distrust the authority of Scripture. Even most of the clergy were persuaded, and thus the situation remains to this day. Today millions of people attend churches each Sunday to engage in a form of worship, but without the teaching of God's Word.

Even among the evangelical churches of America, worship evidences a disregard for God's Word. Sermons vehemently trumpet the preacher's opinion—or merely generate emotion to elicit a desired response—while making little reference to the Scriptures. Many laypersons accept the word of popular Christian authors or radio and television preachers, without checking the Bible for themselves. Christian books and broadcasting are not inherently wrong; the danger lies in the fact that many Christians now allow a favorite personality to be their final arbiter in matters of faith.

In many ways, the world of today is no different from the world of biblical times. Human nature has not changed; people need God as much now as they did then. In the time of Nehemiah, for example, the people of Israel had descended into a profound ignorance of God's Word. After generations of pagan captivity they still retained some of their old religious traditions. But without knowledge of the Scriptures, the people could not worship with understanding.

GATHERED TO HEAR GOD'S WORD

Nehemiah was a trusted official of the Babylonian king in whose land God's people had been exiled for more than fifty years. When Nehemiah heard that Jerusalem had fallen into decay, its gates burned and its walls broken down, he "sat down and wept, and mourned for many days…fasting and praying before the God of heaven" (Neh. 1:4). The Babylonian king had compassion for the sadness of his servant and gave Nehemiah royal authorization and material aid to rebuild the walls.

Despite opposition from local officials who benefited from Jerusalem's weakness, Nehemiah journeyed to the city and rebuilt the walls in just fifty-two days. This amazing feat was completed on the twenty-fifth day of the sixth month on the Jewish calendar (Neh. 6:15). The Bible records that a week later, on the first day of the seventh month,

> All the people gathered together as one man in the open square that was in front of the Water Gate; and they told Ezra the scribe to bring the Book of the Law of Moses, which the LORD had commanded Israel. So Ezra the priest brought the Law before the assembly of men and women and all who could hear with understanding on the first day of the seventh month. Then he read from it in the open square that was in front of the Water Gate from morning until midday, before the men and women and

those who could understand; and the ears of all the people were attentive to the Book of the Law. (Neh. 8:1-3)

This was a special day on the Jewish calendar. For the seventh month was the most important month in the year, a month in which God had ordained that His people should observe various celebrations and practices. On the first day of the month they were to hold the Feast of Trumpets, the nation's New Year celebration, during which they thanked God for past provision and looked forward to future service. The tenth day of the month was the Day of Atonement, upon which the head of every family—as well as all males who had reached the age of accountability—was required to go to Jerusalem and participate in sacrifices for sin. On the fifteenth day, the people were to celebrate the Feast of Tabernacles. In every seventh year at this feast (Deut. 31:10-11), God expected all His people to be called together for the reading of the Law so that "they may hear and that they may learn to fear the LORD your God and carefully observe all the words of this law, and that their children, who have not known it, may hear and learn to fear the LORD your God (Deut. 31:12-13)."

It was perhaps with this custom in mind that the people in Jerusalem gathered together and spontaneously urged Ezra the scribe "to bring the Book of the Law." Although the Feast of Tabernacles was still two weeks away, in their joy at the rebuilding of the walls the people yearned to hear God's Word read to them. It was fitting on this great occasion for them to rehearse God's blessing and praise Him. Besides, the first day of the seventh month was special in its own right as a day of new beginnings, an occasion to rejoice and thank God for His blessings. And so the people asked to hear the words that God commanded His people to hear and know. Do we have the same desire when we gather as His people? Is God's Word important to us, or do we look forward to Sunday merely as a time for seeing our friends and getting an emotional boost?

Consider Nehemiah's description of this great celebration day. The people "gathered themselves together as one man." They had a unity of purpose that was centered on their mutual excitement and hunger for God's Word. As New Testament Christians, we enjoy God's precious promise to feed any of us who have such a hunger.

Jesus said, "Blessed *are* they who hunger and thirst for righteousness, for they shall be filled" (Matt. 5:6).

In the record of the event in Nehemiah 8:1-12, the word "people" occurs thirteen times. The word describes masses of excited people gathered in one place for a purpose. Whole families, not just the fathers, were in attendance. And they listened "attentively" for *six* hours! Many Christian leaders today strive for this kind of mass response. But Nehemiah and Ezra did not need to "pump up" the crowd. The people were not gathered because of any high-pressure appeal or promise of entertainment. Neither had they assembled to observe a dead tradition. They expected to be taught from the Word of God.

So great was this expectation that the people made special preparations so that everyone would hear the instruction. They constructed a large platform for Ezra and his helpers to use in declaring God's Word (8:4). Perhaps this platform was the first pulpit! Beginning from this point in Jewish history, the temple with its sacrifices was no longer the center of religious expression. Instead, families started gathering in synagogues to be taught, to gain understanding of the Torah, to praise God, and to enjoy fellowship.

Nehemiah records also that "the people *stood* in their place" (8: 7). Apparently, men, women, and children all stood on their feet "from the morning until midday" to hear the reading of the Law. Today, of course, we begin to feel uncomfortable when the preacher goes on for more than twenty minutes. But the real point of this narrative detail, however, is not that the people endured a long message, but that they received the message with an attentive attitude. It is possible for you and me to attend church and *hear* God's Word but not to *listen*. The people who gathered at the rebuilt walls of Jerusalem both heard *and* listened! Similarly, Christians who love the Bible yearn to have it explained to them, and so they apply themselves to attentive listening. It is often the case that we get out of a sermon what we put into it!

COMMITTED TO GIVE GOD'S WORD

So far we have looked at the story in Nehemiah from the viewpoint of the people. What about the viewpoint leaders? Put yourself in their place. They faced an excited mass of people gathered "as one man," all clamoring for Ezra to bring the book. Although it seems likely that the leaders had called for the gathering, the people's request to read the law seems to have been spontaneous. The fact that Ezra did not have the book with him, but had to go get it, suggests that the leaders may have had a different purpose for the meeting than that of reading the Scriptures. How did they respond to this change in plans?

The leaders responded by bringing the book and reading the Word. Of course they did! Why should they declare anything other than God's Word in the hearing of God's people? Ezra stood on a platform "above all the people" (8:5) so that everyone could see that the book was open. The other leaders assisted Ezra by going out among the people. They "helped the people to understand the Law; and the people *stood* in their place. So they read distinctly from the book, in the Law of God; and they gave the sense, and helped them to understand the reading" (Neh. 8:7-8).

From their example, we learn that God's leaders must desire for people to hear God's Word. But we learn, too, that it is not always sufficient simply to stand up and read the Bible. Often people need an explanation of the text. God anticipates this need by providing pastors for His Church and teachers for His Church whom He has gifted to divide His Word rightly (Eph. 4:11-12). Since in Nehemiah's day many of the people may have adopted the Aramaic language, the original Hebrew of God's law may have been confusing to them. But the leaders "gave the sense, and helped *them* to understand the reading." This same kind of pulpit ministry may not move people down the aisles, but it does move God's people along in the process of faith and godliness.

When at last the people had heard the Word of God and understood the instruction, they responded in true worship. Ezra stood before the people and publicly affirmed God's greatness. Then all the people agreed with him, raising their hands to the glory of God. They were not praising Ezra, nor were they responding to his clever oratory or opinions. The people gave the glory to God and then, out of humble hearts, they bowed themselves in humble worship.

And Ezra blessed the Lord, the great God. Then all the people answered, "Amen, Amen!" while lifting up their hands. And they bowed their heads and worshiped the Lord with their faces to the ground. (Neh. 8:6)

Nehemiah does not record that there was any music or offerings, at least on this occasion. And though all the people did return home afterward for quiet yet joyful celebration, they celebrated "because they understood the words that were declared to them" (8:12). That understanding is the key. There would be music and offerings on other occasions of worship in the future history of the Jewish people. But, then, just as on the great day when the walls of Jerusalem were rebuilt, true worship could not take place until the people understood the Word of their God.

THINGS TO THINK ABOUT

1. Early Christians studied God's Word (Acts 2:42) when they worshiped. What are some ways in which we have departed from that study?

2. Why did the rebuilding of the walls of Jerusalem cause the people to respond by wanting to hear God's Word?

3. The people listened for six hours! Is it possible for us to *hear* God's Word but not *listen*? If so, how do we avoid this danger?

4. The leaders not only declared God's Word to the people, but also "caused them to understand." How does this principle apply today?

5. Explain in your own words why true worship cannot take place without an understanding of God's Word.

14

TRUE WORSHIP PRAISES GOD'S HOLINESS

THE PSALMIST • PSALM 99

Exalt the Lord our God, and worship at His holy hill; for the Lord our God is holy.

In pastoral counseling I discern much about a couple's relationship by the way they treat each other. If a husband and wife come to my study, sit apart, and fail to look at each other, I conclude that their relationship is strained. Meaningful communication and cooperation have probably stopped. Perhaps it is the man's habit to come home from work and watch TV all night. Perhaps the woman goes out shopping and makes purchases without regard for her husband's approval. There is no partnership any longer because at least one partner has stopped loving the other and has decided to live as he or she pleases without regard to the other's feelings.

The world would say that this couple needs to get the love and romance back in their marriage. But a solid, happy relationship is built in fact on mutual respect. As a Christian you can offer love to another person and not receive love in return. That would constitute a "relationship" of sorts, but not a happy one. But when both parties have a mutual respect for each other, the basis for a positive and satisfying relationship exists.

A solid marriage is a good description of the relationship that must exist between God and His people. Although the Lord is not under any obligation to you and me, He daily earns our respect by the way He treats us. His love and provision for us are steadfast, His grace and mercy infinite. His awesome power is all around for us to see. Even His chastisements are perfect in their justice. He is altogether holy! These attributes characterize how God treats us, but how do we treat Him? Do we treat God in such a way as to earn His respect as His good and faithful servants?

A key barometer of how we treat God is our worship. This fact was true in Old Testament days when God's people sometimes had great respect for God and at other times followed their own ideas. At such times they might still observe the outward forms of worship, or they might forsake appearances and follow after idols. Either way, they forgot about the Lord and failed to treat Him with respect. You and I can do the same thing today when we casually bring all our sinful baggage with us on Sunday, or forget that He is holy, or perhaps do not even truly know the God we claim to worship. Such lack of respect will be evident in our relationship with Him.

THE LORD REIGNS

By contrast to such worship, true worship reveals our respect for His holiness. That is the message of the Ninety-Ninth Psalm which begins,

> The LORD reigns; let the peoples tremble! He dwells between the cherubim; let the earth be moved! The LORD is great in Zion; and He is high above all the peoples. (Ps. 99:1-2)

That men should tremble before God's authority is clear. But to emphasize this truth, the psalmist points out that the Lord dwells among the cherubim. Perhaps this observation is a reference to the tabernacle and God's chosen place of presence at the mercy seat, which rested upon the ark of the covenant. God commanded Moses, "And you shall make two cherubim of gold; of hammered work you shall make them at the two ends of the mercy seat" (Ex. 25:18). This place was so sacred that the high priest could approach it only once a year on the Day of Atonement. Even then, he wore bells on his robe and had a rope tied to him in case God should strike him dead.

The reference to God's sitting "between the cherubim" may also be a reference to His divine nature. Cherubim and seraphim are angelical beings created by God to praise Him. In several passages the Bible describes the cherubim as surrounding God's heavenly throne, attesting to His holiness. "And one cried to another, and said, Holy, holy, holy, is the LORD of hosts: the whole earth is full of His glory" (Is. 6:3). Truly, this is a God who can make the earth to quake at his power and presence!

God reigns, and He is "great in Zion." This is another name for Jerusalem, the city of His choosing, where His *shekinah* glory once graced the tabernacle and then the temple. To say the Lord is great in Zion may be an affirmation that God is great among His people. While He is with them, they are invincible in doing His will.

After the psalmist praises the God who is mighty over the tabernacle and over the city, the progression continues. For the Lord is "high above *all* the people." Even kings cannot compare to His greatness! Yet even as we tremble before Him, we are comforted to know that a God who dwells "above all the people" can see all things. He is in control of every detail of your life and mine, and He cares intensely about His people. A right view of God sees Him in all of the glory that the Bible attributes to Him. Such a view compels us to treat Him with the awesome respect that is His due. When we view His glory we will bow with the psalmist in true worship and declare,

Let them praise Your great and awesome name—He is holy. (Ps. 99:3)

THE LORD IS RIGHTEOUS

The Scriptures affirm that this God who has the power to do *anything* chooses to do the *right* thing. He is not like the capricious deities worshiped by pagan peoples. He does not make right simply by His might. Of God the psalmist sings, "The King's strength also loves justice; You have established equity; You have executed justice and righteousness in Jacob" (Ps.99:4).

God exercises perfect justice every time. He always establishes equitable decisions, always forms righteous plans, and always does justly. Why? Because He is holy. Therefore we are to "exalt the LORD our God, and worship at His footstool—He is holy" (Ps. 99:5).

Because He is God and therefore reigns in perfect equity and justice, you and I must exalt Him. This exaltation presupposes that we truly know God's attributes—and that knowledge comes only through a vibrant personal relationship with Him. Anyone can know *about* God or even use words from the Bible when in worship. But an intellectual knowledge of the Lord is not enough. Even "the demons believe, and tremble" (James 2:19). Those who do not *know* God cannot exalt His attributes. It is for this reason that we often see worship that suggests the worshipers know only a god of wealth or pleasure, or they know only of mere religion. In contrast, true worship lifts up the name of God because the worshipers know Him intimately.

One necessary means of calling proper attention to God is His people's assuming their proper place before Him. The psalmist enjoins us to "worship at His footstool," giving a picture of our obeisance before His kingly throne. Psalms 93 through 99 are in fact called the "Royal Psalms," because they exalt the majestic King Jehovah. Thus we read in Psalm 93,

> The LORD reigns, He is clothed with majesty; the LORD is clothed, He has girded Himself with strength. Surely the world is established, so that it cannot be moved. Your throne is established from of old; You are from everlasting. (vv. 1-2)

Ancient thrones often sat on a platform atop several steps. Once the king had ascended the steps, he could sit on the throne and put his feet on the footstool that was attached to the throne. The footstool existed for his comfort. However, the footstool also became a picture of subservience and subjugation. Sometimes the footstool was carved with the likeness of the king's enemies. When the king put his feet on the stool, everyone was reminded that the king had brought these enemies into subjection.

God's footstool reminds us that He is the King. Many times in the Scriptures we read that God will make of His enemies a footstool.

Other passages state that the Lord has His footstool in the tabernacle, and in others the Lord declares that "the earth is [His] footstool" (Is. 66:1, Acts 7:49). In all these references we are reminded that God is exalted as we worship in our proper place of submission.

Such submission can be joyfully given to God because of His holiness: "Your testimonies are very sure: holiness adorns Your house, O LORD, forever" (Ps. 93:5). God's holiness permits the perfect marriage of might and right. Indeed, God's holiness is the symphony of all of His attributes—attributes that the human mind cannot fully comprehend. God is angry at sin and yet is full of love. He pours out wrath against rebels and yet is altogether longsuffering. His holiness is the glue that joins these attributes together. His strength loves justice. He both establishes equity and executes righteousness. True worship will exalt such a God.

THE LORD IS REVEALED

Having established God's attributes of authority and greatness, justice and righteousness, the psalmist moves on to his application. God's holy nature is revealed through His dealings with humanity. For the Lord rules with equity when He allows His people to pray and intercede for others; when, altogether just, He yet forgives sins; and when also He allows forgiven sinners to reap the full consequences of their sins. In other words, our God is wonderful, forgiving, and gracious—but because He is also just and mighty, the very thought of sin should strike fear in our hearts. Realization of both aspects of God's character helps us understand that God is holy, and this understanding results in true worship to Him.

To illustrate these truths, the psalmist provides instructive examples from the lives of three of God's choice servants.

> Moses and Aaron were among His priests, and Samuel was among those who called upon His name; they called upon the Lord, and He answered them. He spoke to them in the cloudy pillar; they kept His testimonies and the ordinance He gave them. You answered them, O LORD our God; You were to them God-Who-Forgives, though You took vengeance on their deeds. (Ps. 99:6-8)

For serious Bible students, this passage may raise a question: Why is Moses called a priest? God did not ordain the priesthood until He gave the Law, and, in fact, the first priest was Aaron. The Hebrew word here translated "priests," however, actually means to minister or do religious service. And Moses performed priestly work before God ordained the specific institution of the priesthood. Moses even officiated at Aaron's ordination. Also, he was born in the line of Levi, the required lineage for all priests. He interceded between God and the people, thus performing one of the chief functions of priests, and he prayed on behalf of both individuals and the entire nation.

Of course, the emphasis of the passage is not on the credentials of Moses, Aaron, and Samuel. The point is that even these mighty leaders did not hesitate to admit their powerlessness and seek the Lord in prayer. Sometimes He answered immediately, and at other times He answered later. Often the answer was miraculous—as it was when God brought the people out of Egypt in the time of Moses and Aaron, or when He answered Samuel's plea to give Israel victory over superior foes.

God still delights in answering His servants' prayers today. Although He may have spoken "in the cloudy pillar" in days of old, God still speaks to His servants today through His written Word. Now, as then, God is always faithful to tell His servants what they need to know. He is under no obligation to us, but He lovingly desires that we discover His holiness through the instruction He gives. Moses, Aaron, and Samuel provided a further example of heeding such instruction, for they kept God's testimonies and ordinances. Even as a small boy, Samuel answered the Lord's voice by saying, "Speak; for Your servant hears" (1 Sam. 3:10).

But can you and I really take comfort from the fact that God answered the prayers of Moses, Aaron, and Samuel? If these men attained a level of perfection that the rest of us can never hope to reach, their example provides little encouragement. Yet the psalmist points out that even these great men of God struggled with sin just as you and I do. They had weaknesses and failings so that even though God "answered them" and was "to them God-Who-Forgives," He nonetheless "took vengeance on their deeds" (Ps. 99:8)

Moses, Aaron, and Samuel all committed sins against God. The Bible records that Moses incurred the Lord's wrath at the waters of Meribah Kadesh, where he showed lack of respect for God in the presence of the people (Deut. 32:51). Aaron also stirred God's anger at Meribah, and he had earlier transgressed when he sanctioned idol worship (Ex. 32:1-6) and a rebellion against Moses' leadership (Num. 12:1-2). And what was Samuel's sin? We cannot say determinately since the Bible provides no direct mention of it, unless it was perhaps a failure to discipline his two sons (1 Sam. 8:3).

However, we do know two things for certain. First, according to the psalmist, all three men confessed and repented of their failures. How do we know? Moses, Aaron, and Samuel must each have been contrite before the Lord, for He forgave them. Second, notwithstanding His forgiveness, God still (as the King James Bible puts its) took "vengeance of their inventions." That is, when His servants followed their own ways, God allowed even these great men to bear the full consequences of their sin. Both Moses and Aaron, for example, were not permitted to enter the Promised Land. Instead, even with the end of their wilderness journey in sight, God took them to glory (Num. 33:38, Deut. 34:5).

We, too, will stumble and fall into sin. But "if we confess our sins, He is faithful and just to forgive us *our* sins, and to cleanse us from all unrighteousness" (1 John 1:9). Nevertheless, we must always face some kind of consequence because of that sin. Why? Because God is just and holy. Yet there is a second reason, one intended for our benefit. Just as the nerves of our fingertips warn us never again to touch a hot stove, the experience of sin's consequences is an inducement to forsake our own "inventions."

David is perhaps the Bible's greatest illustration of this principle. Although he confessed to sinning with Bathsheba and was forgiven, he reaped the consequences of his sin for the rest of his life. Was God unfair to allow David to feel the consequences of his sin? No, He begged us not to commit those sins. Once we transgress His ways, however, God's holiness demands complete repudiation of that transgression. And when we endure sin's consequences, we begin to have a better understanding of His holiness.

THE LORD IS REVERED

The psalmist has sung of God's holiness as demonstrated by the way He reigns in awesome might, dwells above all the people, combines power with justice, answers prayer, gives instruction, and forgives sin though not disallowing its consequences. So what is the natural conclusion of the matter? The psalmist exhorts us to "exalt the LORD our God, and worship at His holy hill; for the LORD our God is holy" (Ps. 99:9).

To exalt means to lift up. Does God then *need* me to lift Him up? Of course not. Read what the psalmist has written. You and I should exalt the Holy One, not just because He is God, but because He is *our* God! If we are His people, we lift up our God's name above all others. Think about it! He is altogether holy, and yet we who are nothing by comparison can call Him *our* God! Considering our God and ourselves in that light, our natural expression must be to give Him the highest place in all things. And if He holds that place, our worship should show it.

God's preeminence is the reason we join with the psalmist in worshiping at God's holy hill, His prescribed place of worship. Yes, God is present wherever "two or three are gathered together in My name" (Matt. 18:20). Yet in the law that God gave to Moses, He promised there would be a place appointed where the people must go to worship. That place was wherever the ark of the covenant was located (with the exception of the brief time that it was in the hands of the Philistines). God's promise to His people was this:

> And there I will meet with you, and I will speak with you from
> above the mercy seat, from between the two cherubim which are
> on the ark of the Testimony (Ex. 25:22)

At first, this promise meant that the place of worship was the tabernacle that God's people put up and took down as they traveled in the wilderness. Later the permanent temple in Jerusalem became the place of worship. Thus, as the psalmist sang in his opening stanzas, the people were called to honor the King who "sits between the cherubim" and to worship Him who is "great in Zion" and "high above all the people."

In the New Testament, God commands us as His people to worship in our hearts. Indeed, even as we learned from the story of Cain and Abel, the heart has always been the site of true worship. Even when God promised to be present in a physical location, He warned the Israelites, "But if your heart turns away so that you do not hear, [you] are drawn away, and worship other gods, and serve them" (Deut. 30:17). Jesus, also, affirmed that true worship takes place in the inner man. He taught that "true worshipers shall worship the Father in spirit and in truth" (John 4:23).

If you and I know God and enjoy His presence in our hearts, we will worship Him there. Our worship and exaltation of Him will manifest humility in response to His holiness. To worship otherwise is to indicate that we do not really know the holy God of the Bible.

THINGS TO THINK ABOUT

1. How is God's holiness shown through His *position* as the One who reigns and who is great and high?

2. How is God's holiness shown through his *perfection* in miraculously combining both might and right?

3. What does it mean to you personally to "worship at His footstool, for He is holy"? How would you apply this command?

4. Why does God pardon your sins but also allow you to endure the consequences of those sins?

5. Considering the truth of God's holiness, what does it mean to you to worship not just the fact that God exists, but to worship Him as *your* God?

15

TRUE WORSHIP
BOWS IN HUMILITY

THE MAGI • MATTHEW 2:1-12

And when they had come into the house, they saw the young
Child with Mary His mother, and fell down, and worshiped
Him: and…they presented gifts to Him.

D o you know more about God today than you did when you were first born again? You should. In the months and years since your spiritual birth, you have had the opportunity to know God more intimately through reading His Word and experiencing His daily fellowship. Theologians use the term *sanctification* to describe the process of growing into a deeper knowledge of and relationship with God. For the Christian, such growth should be the norm. Even the Bible itself is a picture of this process of growth. A chronological study of the Scriptures shows that, over time, God continually revealed more and more about Himself.

Theologians call this ever-increasing revelation the *progress of doctrine*. In terms of this concept, the generation of Moses, for example, would be more responsible for worshiping God properly than would previous generations. The written law God gave to Moses explained His holy requirements in clear detail so that His people would be without excuse. We who have the entire Bible are held even more responsible to offer true worship to God.

Sadly, however, we often fail in our responsibility. Despite having God's written law, the Jews at times went so far as to worship false gods, and today we repeat the same tragedy. We worship pleasure and power and plenty. But ours is a more grievous transgression than was theirs. Since we have the entire Word of God, the magnitude of our failure is all the greater.

Possession of facts, then, does not always produce true worship. Consider the story of Christ's birth. The record of Matthew portrays how three different kinds of people responded to the same set of facts. King Herod feared being replaced by a new king and responded with animosity to Christ. The Jewish chief priests and scribes were indifferent toward Christ because they had their own plans regarding religion. But the Magi, who probably knew least about the Messiah, were the ones who worshiped and adored God the Son.

Three responses—animosity, apathy, adoration. These responses still compose the range of responses we see toward Christ in our world today. Which one characterizes you and me?

ANIMOSITY TOWARD TRUE WORSHIP

Although King Herod possessed a certain knowledge of the prophecies summoning the Jewish Messiah, Herod was not really one of God's people. He reigned as the Jews' local king, but he was actually a usurper of the throne. Julius Caesar had appointed Herod's father as governor of Judea when Rome occupied the region in 47 B.C., and the father appointed his son Herod as prefect of Galilee. Seven years later Judea was invaded and occupied by the Parthians. Herod escaped to Rome where the emperor agreed to make Herod king of the Jews if he could defeat the Parthians. This Herod did, leading an army back to Galilee and expelling the Parthians in 36 B.C.

Herod was an Idumean and therefore descended from the Edomites, a people who had been the Jews' enemies for centuries. To boost his credentials Herod married a woman from a leading Jewish family. And to better manipulate his subjects, Herod familiarized himself with the Jewish laws and religious hierarchy. He tried to work with the Sadducees and Pharisees, and even rebuilt the Jerusalem temple so that it was larger and more magnificent than Solomon's temple. But though he knew about their laws, understood their religious system, and built them a greater temple, Herod was not a worshiper of the true God.

Herod could not worship Christ because he worshiped himself. Herod killed his wife and her family because their power threatened his. He killed his own sons when he suspected they might try to take his throne. Even his "good" deeds were cynical attempts to secure his own popularity. On the one hand, he rebuilt the temple to please the people's religious sensibilities. And once during a famine, he gave gifts to the poor. But on the other hand, he built racetracks, theaters, and public baths for the people's entertainment and pleasure. Herod did not do these things because he loved the people. He did them because he wanted to buy the people off.

Herod was a man who knew some religious truth and even did some seemingly religious things. When the Magi showed up at his court, he professed an interest in the Christ child. He called a meeting with the religious leaders in order to gather information about the Messiah from the Scriptures (Matt. 2:4). He instructed the Magi to "go and search carefully for the young Child, and when you have found Him, bring back word to me, that I may come and worship Him also" (2:8).

In our churches today, Herod might be called a "seeker" and welcomed to join in worship. He knew a smattering of truth and tried to do apparently kind deeds for others. He talked about Jesus in what seemed to be an approving manner, and he tried to gain more information about Him from the Bible. Yet in his heart, he could not allow anyone to rule his life.

Perhaps Herod was wary of the Magi. As we will read later, these wise men may very well have come from Parthia, the same nation that Herod had defeated, to seize his throne in Galilee. It is easy to imagine the displeasure Herod might have felt as this group of Parthian nobles came into his palace and asked about the birth of a new king. And who was this prophesied King of the Jews? Herod most certainly would not submit himself to the Christ child, even if He truly were the Son of God. Herod's real desire was to eliminate Christ from his life—a desire he tried to fulfill, quite literally, by ordering the slaughter of all male infants in Bethlehem (Matt. 2:16-18).

Today, there are those who sit in church pews and feign worship of Christ in order to conceal the truth about themselves. Despite outward appearances, in their hearts they do not want Christ to rule over them. They might be religious, but they do not humbly bow before Christ.

APATHY TOWARD TRUE WORSHIP

The chief priests portray the second type of response to Christ. They possessed great knowledge about the Messiah. Yet despite that knowledge and despite their leadership of God's people, the chief priests did not always toe the line. They were supposed to be descended from the family of Levi, and more specifically from Aaron. But by the time Christ was born, the priests at times served in defiance of this requirement. God also required that only one chief priest serve at a time, and that he held a lifetime appointment. Yet that rule, too, was breached among the religious leaders in Jerusalem.

The chief priests actually had a nice retirement system in place. A man would serve as chief priest for a few years, make good money, and then retire. The retired chief priests, however, still maintained a strong influence among the people. Serving as priest had become a "family business" of sorts. Luke records that "Annas and Caiaphas were high priests" at the time John the Baptist began his ministry (Luke 3:2). Usually we read that verse without ever stopping to think that it reveals a breach of God's law.

The chief priest governed the Sanhedrin, or council of Jewish religious elders. But his most significant function was to go into the Holy of Holies once each year on the Day of Atonement. On that occasion he would sprinkle the blood of the sacrifice on the mercy seat. In Jesus' lifetime, however, this job had become more of a political function than a spiritual one. The chief priest usually belonged, in fact, to the sect of the Sadducees, who were more concerned about politics than sacrifices and offerings.

The scribes, too, were important leaders. They were the most learned persons among the Jews. Usually the scribes were more conservative than the chief priests were, and most belonged to the sect of the Pharisees. These men studied and interpreted God's law all the time, even creating laws intended to aid the people as they implemented God's law. The scribes considered themselves protectors of God's law.

So the chief priests and scribes knew the Scriptures well. When the Magi appeared on the scene and Herod wanted some answers, he knew whom to call.

> And when he had gathered all the chief priests and scribes of the people together, he inquired of them where the Christ was to be born. So they said to him, "In Bethlehem of Judea, for thus it is written by the prophet: 'But you, Bethlehem, in the land of Judah, are not the least among the rulers of Judah; for out of you shall come a Ruler Who will shepherd My people Israel.'" (Matt. 2:4-6)

Herod was not disappointed by the religious leaders' performance. The chief priests and scribes knew immediately the answer to the king's question and cited Micah's prophecy of the Messiah's birthplace. Indeed, the priests and scribes talked often about Messiah. Yet their knowledge about Christ was not evidence of a desire for Him. These religious leaders wanted a Christ of their own making, one who would rule according to their own fashion. Like Herod, therefore, the chief priests and scribes were not genuinely interested in finding the Christ and truly worshiping Him.

These men were too busy worshiping their own religious system. Their system was effective, giving an outward appearance of worship but serving in reality to keep the people under their control. Jesus Himself confronted the chief priests and scribes about this issue. Speaking of the religious leaders, He said,

> They bind heavy burdens, hard to bear, and lay them on men's shoulders; but they themselves will not move them with one of their fingers....But woe to you, scribes and Pharisees, hypocrites! For you shut up the kingdom of heaven against men; for you neither go in yourselves, nor do you allow those who are entering to go in. (Matt. 23:4,13)

The chief priests and scribes did not desire the coming of the true Christ of the Scriptures. He would interrupt their system! The Sadducees, with their concern for politics, wanted a Messiah simply so that he would release them from Roman rule. But unless Messiah's deliverance was a sure thing, the Sadducess preferred to rely on their human abilities to negotiate with Rome. Above all, these leaders feared losing their authority with the people—a fact that became increasingly obvious as Jesus embarked on His earthly ministry.

We scoff at the foolishness of these religious leaders who rejected the very centerpiece of the religion they professed. But are they so different from many of us today? Oh, we have our system honed to perfection. We have our human methods for manipulating the people's emotions, whether through grand traditions or grand performances. And so with our hold upon the people, we do great works and build great religious organizations. To submit ourselves in humility before the authority of Christ would strip away our pretensions and destroy our plans. Although we may know much *about* Christ—and do not hesitate to use Him to achieve our goals—we cannot *submit* to Him. In thus failing to submit, we worship ourselves while claiming to worship Christ.

ADORATION IN TRUE WORSHIP

Compared to the Jewish religious leaders, and even compared to Herod, the Magi possessed a very limited knowledge of Christ. They came from a location east of Judea, very likely from among the Parthians, and they were political and spiritual leaders among their people.

As a class of nobles, the magi first appear in history among the Medes, about one hundred years before the destruction of Jerusalem in 586 B.C. They were the wise men of their society, known to practice sorcery and study the stars. The magi were so important that some referred to them as the "king makers," and, indeed, part of their responsibility was to affirm kings and rulers.

But where did the Magi, those wise men who journeyed to Jerusalem, learn of Christ? Remember that Daniel had served among the magi when Darius was king of Persia. Although the politicians hated Daniel and had him tossed into the lions' den, the Scriptures indicate that his fellow wise men respected him. They were aware of his prophecies and influenced by his dedication to the true God. It is likely, then, that the magi passed down to their successors some of the Old Testament prophecies about a promised Messiah. In addition to Daniel's influence was that of the Jews who remained in Babylon even after Jerusalem was rebuilt. The Jews' testimony thus remained in the Medo-Persian empire.

In the gospel narrative, one thing about the Magi stands out— and it is *not* the image of them presented in our Christmas traditions, an image which is actually rooted in a medieval legend about three Oriental kings. (In fact, there might have been quite an entourage with the Magi, including soldiers!) The important thing to note about the Magi is that, though their knowledge was limited, they responded to what knowledge they possessed. These God-fearing Gentiles saw a special star that indicated to them the birth of the King of Jews. So they set out to follow that star—not because they were obsessed with astrology but because they were trying to find God's King.

What was this star? Astronomers have speculated endlessly about the answer to this question. But to theologians, or to anyone who reads the gospel accounts, it is clear that God supplied the star's light. The record of Matthew suggests that the star disappeared before the Magi reached Jerusalem. Naturally, therefore, they stopped at the capital city to inquire about the Jewish king. Then, after their visit to Herod, "they departed."

> And behold, the star which they had seen in the East went before them, till it came and stood over where the young Child was. When they saw the star, they rejoiced with exceedingly great joy. And when they had come into the house, they saw the young Child with Mary His mother, and fell down and worshiped Him. (Matthew 2:9-11a)

Put yourself in the Magi's sandals. You have journeyed far, and travel is difficult and dangerous. Then the star you have followed in the hope of finding God's King seemingly disappears. You stop in Jerusalem to obtain more detailed information about this king. King Herod, upon the advice of the religious authorities, sends you to Bethlehem. Now at least you have some information to go on. Then, miraculously and unexpectedly, the star reappears! You are elated! This bright light is God's unique revelation to you, and you respond to His leading. In the end, the light leads you to the very house where the Christ child lies. God is so faithful! And if this King is yet a child, you know He is divine. You are overcome with a fearful and wonderful awe. It is only natural that the expression of your heart is to "fall down and worship Him."

This is the response of those who are sincere with God and who follow His leading. The Magi went to Bethlehem to worship the Savior. They found Him because God led them to the spot. And when they found Him, they bowed in submission and humbly adored Him.

Churches are full of people who may have some knowledge about Christ but (like Herod) maintain a false front for their own ends, or (like the religious leaders) are satisfied with their system and do not want the real Christ to mess it up. Few are the people who, like the Magi, humbly bow before Christ and offer Him all that they have. But these are the true worshipers.

THINGS TO THINK ABOUT

1. What is the concept of the "progress of doctrine"? What standard of accountability does this concept impose on Christians today?

2. King Herod had some knowledge of Scripture, did some good deeds, and seemed to speak approvingly of Christ. Then how could Herod actually bear *animosity* toward the Savior?

3. Of the three groups who responded to Christ in some way, the chief priests and scribes knew the most about Scripture. Why then did they regard Christ with *apathy*?

4. The Magi knew the least about Scripture. Why then was their response to Christ one of *adoration*?

5. Do we still find these three responses to Christ—animosity, apathy, adoration—in the church today? Why do they exist?

16

TRUE WORSHIP DESIRES GOD'S WAY

THE DISCIPLES • MATTHEW 14:22-33

And when they got into the boat, the wind ceased. Then those who were in the boat came and worshiped Him, saying, "Truly You are the Son of God."

Occasionally I observe the signs in front of various churches around town. "Casual Worship," some proclaim to passersby. Of course, it is true that Christ invites all men to "come as they are" and find Him. "If anyone thirsts, let him come to Me and drink" (John 7:37). Yet the idea of *casual worship* is perhaps one of the greatest oxymorons in the church today. How can anyone who truly believes in the Almighty God of the universe approach His worship casually?

Sadly, the notion of "casual worship" makes perfect sense in our culture today. Americans have made an art form of staying in their comfort zones. Being secure, peaceful, and happy is the American way. Schools teach children to practice tolerance for all moral choices rather than to stand on principle. Many adults would rather lie or cheat than face difficulties. And as Christians we, too, have our comfort zones.

Being a history buff, I have often toured early American churches. Invariably, visitors at these historic churches disdain the seeming arrogance of colonial families who paid money to rent certain pews. But as a pastor, I observe how modern families mark off "their" seats (and parking spaces) almost as securely as if they had been rented. At our church we make a conscious effort to change the order of service occasionally and to learn unfamiliar hymns, to avoid becoming "too" comfortable. Even so, we have developed our own comfortable set of traditions over the years.

All churches fall into these patterns. It is only human to desire the security of familiar things. But in our desire to avoid discomfort, are we sometimes willing to cross the line into questionable worship practices? If so (and I believe it is so), is our relationship with God perhaps more shallow than we want to admit?

To put the issue another way, does God ever intend for His people to be *uncomfortable?* Yes! For discomfort is one way that God can draw us closer to Himself. People who trust God through hardship learn to trust Him implicitly—and their trust shows in their worship. Christian believers in former communist countries, for example, need not be begged to attend worship services. America itself once knew such a deep level of worship: many of our forebears left all familiar comforts behind to practice pure religion in a New World. Their worship was on a plane that most American Christians today have never experienced. These men and women risked their lives and fortunes to learn more of Christ.

The worship of our Christian forebears proved the depth of their experience with Christ. What does our worship today say about us? I fear that much of our worship declares that we love comfort and convenience. But there is a better way of worship, a way that is modeled for us in the Scriptures by the disciples of Jesus.

LEARNING OF JESUS' AUTHORITY

Staying within our comfort zones is, at root, the desire to have our own way. True worship, however, involves a desire for God to have *His* way. The personal autonomy of the worshiper must be yielded to the authority of the One being worshiped. The disciples saw this principle in action immediately following one of the most famous events recorded in the New Testament, the miracle of the loaves and fishes.

Then He commanded the multitudes to sit down on the grass. And He took the five loaves and the two fish, and looking up to heaven, He blessed and broke and gave the loaves to the disciples; and the disciples gave to the multitudes. So they all ate and were filled, and they took up twelve baskets full of the fragments that remained. Now those who had eaten were about five thousand men, besides women and children. (Matt. 14:19-21)

Immediately following this miracle, however, something surprising happened. Jesus did not use the miracle as an opportunity to get the crowd's attention, to continue His teaching, or to recruit new followers. Instead, "immediately Jesus made His disciples get into the boat, and go before Him to the other side [of the lake], while he sent the multitudes away" (Matt. 14:22). Jesus told the people to go home!

Imagine yourself in the disciples' place. The Scriptures imply that their boat was still close enough to shore for the disciples to see Jesus dismissing the multitude. In fact, the disciples probably hung around to watch Him doing so. They were likely astonished at their Master's actions. Earlier that day Jesus, moved by compassion, had come to the people and "healed their sick" (14:14). Since then, the crowd had listened intently to Jesus' teaching. How intently? So intently that they remained with Jesus in "a deserted place" far from their villages. The people remained late into the night, beyond the time of their evening meal, so that they experienced a legitimate need for food (14:15).

Jesus met that need by providing food in a miraculous way. How did the people react to His provision? In John's account we read that the people proclaimed Jesus to be the fulfillment of divine prophecy and declared their desire for Him to lead them. From the perspective the twelve disciples, this response would have seemed like a positive development. But Jesus saw something entirely different.

Those men, when they had seen the sign that Jesus did, said, "This is truly the Prophet who is to come into the world." Therefore when Jesus perceived that they were about to come and take Him by force to make Him king, He departed. (John 6:14-15)

The people obviously did not understand God's way. But God the Son, knowing the plans of God the Father, refused to let the crowd draw Him out of the Father's will. Thus with authority He dismissed the people.

So it is in our own day. Much of the time most of us do not understand God's way. Was the miracle of the loaves and fishes any more awesome than the way God has blessed *us*? In America today we enjoy an unprecedented standard of living. What other nation has ever achieved a higher standard? Our citizens who live in poverty often enjoy more material provision than the average person in many other countries around the world. Sadly, however, we often react to our wonderful blessings by trying to draft Jesus into our own plans. We demand that Jesus be the kind of king that *we* want. Like the people in the gospel accounts, we too could use a lesson in the authority of Jesus.

Jesus taught His disciples the same lesson that He taught the crowd; He dismissed them too! "Get in the boat," He told them in essence, "then go to the other side and wait! I'm going to be alone for a while." So indeed, "When He had sent the multitudes away, He went up on the mountain by Himself to pray. Now when evening came, He was alone there." (Matt. 14:23)

The disciples had preferred to stay around and enjoy the excitement. Things were really starting to happen! If there were "five thousand men, besides women and children" (Matt. 14:21), then the entire crowd likely numbered twenty thousand! The miracle of feeding so many people was awesome and the zeal of such a large multitude was tantalizing. Because the disciples were the inner circle, they would be rulers with Christ when He was king. Why was Jesus making them leave this place of such apparent blessing? And why did they have to get in a boat, alone, and go out on the sea in the darkness of night?

We can conclude that the disciples were distracted by the excitement surrounding this miracle because Jesus had to *constrain* them (14:22) to get into the boat. The Greek wording indicates resistance on the part of Jesus' disciples; Jesus had to insist that they leave. Nevertheless, because the disciples respected Jesus' authority, they submitted to Him.

Jesus directed the disciples to go across the northern part of the lake to the town of Capernaum (according to John) or nearby

Genesaret (according to Mark), making a short trip of about two miles. Their full submission is illustrated, too, by their perseverance to follow instructions despite a storm that blew them three or four miles out to sea. We find them some six to nine hours later, still struggling to get the boat to the right destination. It would have been easier to ride out the storm and land wherever the winds took them. But the disciples wanted to obey Jesus, so they fought the storm.

This lesson is one we, too, need to learn. The path God tells us to walk is not always easy. The temptation to take another path can be great. Yet God has a plan for us, one He has devised for our benefit and edification. If we do not submit to His authority, we will miss His plan. If we miss His plan, we will not learn the things that we should. True worship is expressed only by those who have learned through obedience that Jesus is their authority.

LEARNING OF JESUS' CARE

Perhaps you have noticed what might seem to be a problem with Matthew's account. The miracle of the loaves and fishes occurred "when it was evening" (14:15) and the disciples suggested to Jesus that He send the multitude home to eat. But *after* the miraculous feeding and Jesus' dismissal of the crowd, Jesus went alone to pray "when evening came" (14:23). How could it still be evening?

In fact, the Jews had *two* evenings. One evening lasted from three to six in the afternoon, and the second from six to nine. Jesus went to pray during the second evening.

As the account continues, we learn of Jesus' great care and concern for His disciples. As Mark relates the story, "when He had sent [the multitude] away, He departed to the mountain to pray."

> Now when evening came, the boat was in the middle of the sea; and He was alone on the land. Then He saw them straining at rowing, for the wind was against them. And about the fourth watch of the night He came to them, walking on the sea. (Mark 6:46-48)

The fourth watch would have been about three o'clock in the morning. The disciples had been fighting the storm all night and knew they were in trouble. Why had the Master put them in this predicament? If He knew the storm was coming, why had He not come with them? If Jesus could see His disciples from the mountain, why did He not come to them right away? Why did He wait?

We still ask these same questions today!

Jesus waited so that the disciples could learn. He waited to go to Lazarus for the same reason. That principle remains true today; God often waits in order to give us opportunity to learn more about Him. But at last, Jesus came to the disciples' aid.

> Now in the fourth watch of the night Jesus went to them, walking on the sea. And when the disciples saw Him walking on the sea, they were troubled, saying, "It is a ghost!" And they cried out for fear. But immediately Jesus spoke to them, saying, "Be of good cheer! It is I; do not be afraid." (Matt. 14:25-27)

The fact that the disciples had much to learn about Jesus' care for them is seen in their reaction to His appearing. How could they be troubled and fearful, thinking Jesus was a ghost? They were afraid because the men were not expecting Jesus. They imagined the worst because their thoughts were not on Christ. So the Master had to tell the disciples to be cheerful rather than afraid. Like the disciples, we can be assured that God will never send us into a trial where He cannot see us.

Jesus revealed through this trial that He cared for His disciples not only as a group, but also individually. His care for His individual disciple evidences itself in His dealings with Peter.

> And Peter answered Him and said, "Lord, if it is You, command me to come to You on the water." So He said, "Come." And when Peter had come down out of the boat, he walked on the water to go to Jesus. But when he saw that the wind was boisterous, he was afraid; and beginning to sink he cried out, saying, "Lord, save me!" And immediately Jesus stretched out His hand and caught him, and said to him, "O you of little faith, why did you doubt?" (Matt. 14:28-31)

Impulsive Peter simply wanted to be near his Lord. He was not sinning or being arrogant or trying to prove something in wanting to walk out on the water to Jesus. By accepting Jesus' invitation, Peter gained an opportunity to learn more about trust. When he put his eyes on the circumstances instead of on Christ, he started sinking in the water. Thus Jesus, in His care for Peter, was able to expose the littleness of Peter's faith (although that faith was superior to anything the other disciples showed). Through his desperate circumstance, Peter was brought to complete trust in Christ. For us as well, that "sinking feeling" is well worth it when we are driven to trust fully in our Lord.

LEARNING OF JESUS' POWER

Peter cried for help, and Jesus saved him from destruction. Peter had to depend fully on Jesus' help, because there was nothing that he could do to help himself. He was powerless. The other disciples were powerless.

When we are insisting on our own way, being powerless seems like a tragedy. But when we yield to God's way—when we step out of our comfort zones—then being powerless is an opportunity. For through our own powerlessness, we can learn of God's power.

> And when they got into the boat, the wind ceased. Then those who were in the boat came and worshiped Him, saying, "Truly You are the Son of God." (Matt. 14:32-33)

During an earlier storm described by Matthew, the disciples implored Christ to aid them and "He arose, and rebuked the winds and the sea; and there was a great calm" (Matt. 8:26). But this time, He spoke no command. The storm was dismissed simply by Christ's presence. He simply came near the disciples and the storm was gone.

So ended a very eventful day! First was a gathering of twenty thousand people, then a miracle feeding, then a night of terror on the sea—and then yet another miracle as Christ walked upon the waters and stilled the storm. The day had not fallen out the way the disciples expected. They were certainly taken out of their comfort zones. But through it all they learned of—and submitted themselves to—Christ's authority, care, and power. The natural expression of their hearts was to "worship him, saying, 'truly You are the Son of God!'" Before this storm, they might have desired to be co-rulers with the king of the multitude. Now they offered true worship to their sovereign, loving, and mighty Lord.

A few years ago, a group in Israel was seeking permission to build a cement walkway that would stand about six inches under the water and extend about a hundred feet out into the Sea of Galilee. Why? So that tourists could pay money to experience walking on water! That kind of experience is exactly what God does *not* want for us. He allows us to have trials so that we might learn of Christ and trust Him more.

Jesus did not come to the disciples in the storm in order to teach them to walk on water. Peter tried that and failed. Rather, Christ came to the disciples in order to encourage them to trust Him in the tough times. Peter learned that lesson. He wrote, "In this you greatly rejoice,"

> Though now for a little while, if need be, you have been grieved by various trials, that the genuineness of your faith, being much more precious than gold that perishes, though it is tested by fire, may be found to praise, honor, and glory at the revelation of Jesus Christ. (1 Peter 1:6-7)

THINGS TO THINK ABOUT

1. God sometimes intends for His people to be *un*comfortable. Give an example of how this fact has been true in your own life.

2. How did the people's plan to make Jesus their king differ from God's plan? What is the cause of the difference?

3. Are we today like the people who saw Jesus' feeding of the five thousand? How do we react to the abundance He has given us?

4. Jesus made the disciples wait before He came to them in the storm. What do you think they learned by having to wait?

5. They experienced multitudes, the miracle, and the storm. Explain in your own words why, in the end, the disciples could worship in truth.

True Worship Can Be Obscured By Tradition

The Scribes and Pharisees • Matthew 15:1-9

And in vain they worship me, teaching as doctrines the
commandments of men.

Many people reject evangelical Christianity because, in their minds, it involves a highly emotional style of worship. In the view of some, "evangelical" services might run the gamut from pulpit pounding on the one hand, to shouting, dancing, and loud music on the other. Church worship, these critics believe, (even if they do not go themselves), should be dignified. A religious service should take place in a venerable sanctuary, accompanied by beautiful organ music and robed choirs singing lofty anthems, and by a priest or minister in vestments who offers a spiritual homily from behind a richly carved pulpit.

Do these things compose true Christian worship? Millions around the world think so. Or at least, if asked to give their idea of worship, they would describe such a scene.

Actually, what the masses call "traditional" worship can be just as far from God's design as are some of the more extreme and deviant "contemporary" practices we see today. The Bible does not teach that tradition should be the standard for true worship. In fact, as we will learn, traditions can stifle true worship just as quickly and effectively as heresy can. As Christians we must guard against substituting mere tradition for true worship. Jesus taught us why when He confronted the issue of traditionalism.

THE TRADITIONALISTS CONFRONTED JESUS

Matthew's gospel records that "the scribes and Pharisees who were from Jerusalem came to Jesus, saying, 'Why do Your disciples transgress the tradition of the elders? For they do not wash their hands when they eat bread'" (15:1-2).

The people who came to Jesus with this question about tradition were not insignificant people. They were the religious authorities among all the Israelites. They were the leaders who determined the standard of worship for God's people—or at least they thought this was their responsibility.

But just who were the scribes? Who were the Pharisees?

The scribes were a body of scholars who interpreted Scripture and, based on their interpretations, wrote laws for God's people to keep. This group of scholars first came into existence when Israel was exiled in Babylon. Israel had been disobedient toward God for many generations. So in keeping with His promise, God allowed the stronger nation of Babylon to carry Israel into captivity and destroy their society.

As a result of the exile, the people's mode of worship was destroyed. Since there was no longer a temple, the priesthood and sacrificial system were gone. No doubt many people determined, therefore, that someone had to maintain the standards of true worship to God. Among the first of the scribes was Ezra, a man who genuinely desired to honor God (Ezra 7:10). Ezra's example might indicate that the early scribes were sincere.

Over time, this initial group of scribes developed into a cohesive body. They established synagogues where Jews met to pray, worship, and learn the law. And they wrote hundreds of laws to help the people keep God's law.

The Pharisees also were leaders of God's people and part of the ruling body called the Sanhedrin. In fact, they made up the most conservative wing of the Sanhedrin. They were determined to keep the laws which the scribes invented and thus protect the scriptures. Their position stood in contrast to that of the more liberal Sadducees, who were not very greatly interested in the traditions.

These are the people—the scribes and Pharisees—who came up from Jerusalem to confront Jesus. They came all the way to Galilee, even though there were local synagogue rulers in Galilee who normally handled questions about the Law or the Scriptures. But apparently these local rulers called for help from the chief authorities in Jerusalem.

This confrontation between Jesus and the religious leaders probably occurred in April, during the third year of Jesus' public ministry. By this time, confrontations between Jesus and the Jewish leaders were becoming more frequent. To the scribes and Pharisees, it was becoming very clear that Jesus' teaching opposed the accepted traditional standards. Thus the leaders posed to Jesus this question: "Why do Your disciples transgress the tradition of the elders?"

The issue on which they chose to confront Jesus was the tradition of hand washing during meals. Were they worried about hygiene? Yes, hygiene was one reason for hand washing. But the leaders did not make the long trip north from Jerusalem to Galilee because they heard that the disciples were being careless and spreading disease. Their concern was for the *ceremonial* aspect of the tradition.

The religious leaders believed that to implement God's command of personal holiness it was necessary to avoid contact with anything the Scriptures might deem unclean. Eating was especially worrisome since it involved touching hand to mouth. A person who touched an unclean item and then touched his mouth, it was claimed, transferred the guilt into his whole body. Thus every Jew was expected to observe an elaborate hand-washing ceremony before and after eating.

But it was not this one ceremony, however, that was the leaders' main concern. The question of hand washing was only one instance of a bigger problem. For the larger issue of their very authority was at stake!

The traditions of the elders, such as ceremonial hand washing, had been passed down orally through the generations of leaders.

These traditions consisted of four elements: oral laws that Moses was supposed to have given in addition to the written laws; decisions made and precedents of judges; explanations and opinions of noted teachers; and votes of the Sanhedrin.

This body of tradition was codified in the late second century after the birth of Christ. Scholars then produced the *Mishnah* (a book of eight hundred pages), which summarized the hundreds of traditional regulations. Later, to explain the *Mishnah,* scholars developed commentaries, which they called *Talmuds*. The Jerusalem Talmud is twelve volumes and the Babylonian Talmud sixty volumes! Obviously, the religious leaders were very serious about their rules. In fact, the Jerusalem Talmud states, "The words of the Scribes are more lovely than the words of the law; for the words of the law are weighty and light, but the words of the Scribes are all weighty."

Although the *Mishnah* was not yet written when the scribes and Pharisees confronted Jesus, the oral traditions it codified were in full force. In accusing His disciples of ignoring the teachings of tradition, the leaders were actually accusing the Teacher who gave the disciples such an example. In the leaders' minds, Jesus and not the disciples was the root of the problem.

JESUS CONFRONTED THE TRADITIONALISTS

Christ had an immediate response to their veiled accusation: "Why do you also transgress the commandment of God because of your tradition?" (Matt. 15:3). Now Jesus was turning the tables on the scribes and Pharisees by citing one of their laws that clearly contradicted God's law.

> For God commanded, saying, "Honor your father and your mother"; and, "He who curses father or mother, let him be put to death." But you say, "Whoever says to his father or mother, 'Whatever profit you might have received from me is a gift to God'—then he need not honor his father or mother." Thus you have made the commandment of God of no effect by your tradition. (Matt. 15:4-6)

Jesus stated God's standard. God clearly commands His people to honor their parents and forbids us to speak disrespectfully of them (Ex. 20:12, 21:17). And since God forbids wrong speaking, He certainly forbids wrong actions. God's standard obviously prohibits us from doing anything that fails to honor our parents.

Yet the scribes and Pharisees held to a tradition that contradicted God's command. This tradition allowed a person to pronounce that any of his possessions were *Corban* (see Mark 7:11), a gift from God that was dedicated to His use. A person could even pronounce a blanket oath over *everything* he owned.

Complete dedication to God is, of course, a correct attitude. But the religious leaders developed the tradition of *Corban* so that they could decline to help needy parents. If their possessions were dedicated to God, after all, they could not take these things away from God and give them to mom or dad! What was worse, the tradition allowed people to continue using their possessions for themselves even after they pronounced them *Corban*. This practice was a common one in New Testament times.

"All too well you reject the commandment of God, that you may keep your tradition," Jesus declares in Mark's account (7:1-13) of the confrontation. And twice in this passage Jesus points out that "many such things you do."

JESUS EXPOSED THE PROBLEM

These leaders presented an appearance of righteousness, but Jesus ripped away their religious facade. "You hypocrites!" He called the scribes and Pharisees—and then He went straight to the cause of their hypocrisy.

> Well did Isaiah prophesy about you, saying: "These people draw
> near to Me with their mouth, And honor Me with their lips, But
> their heart is far from Me." (Matt. 15:7-8)

Jesus here quotes Isaiah (Is. 29:13), who compared the people's spiritual blindness to a closed book. The root problem for these religious hypocrites, Jesus says, is their failure to honor God from their hearts, not just with their words. As a result of their failure, "In vain they worship Me, teaching as doctrines the commandments of men" (Matt. 15:9). Drawing a contrast to the scribes and Pharisees who were obsessive about unclean food, Jesus turned to the gathered crowd and to His disciples, saying,

> Not what goes into the mouth defiles a man; but what comes out of the mouth, this defiles a man....Do you not yet understand that whatever enters the mouth goes into the stomach and is eliminated? But those things which proceed out of the mouth come from the heart, and they defile a man. For out of the heart proceed evil thoughts, murders, adulteries, fornications, thefts, false witness, blasphemies. These are the things which defile a man, but to eat with unwashed hands does not defile a man. (Matt. 15:11,17-21)

Jesus concluded that the religious leaders' worship was vain and empty. That is not to say that the scribes and Pharisees did not worship. They worshiped a great deal. They were very busy. But their worship was not honoring to God, and so it was pointless. Their hearts were not right; they were giving honor to the traditions of men rather than to the God they professed to serve.

Each week, untold multitudes go to church for reasons other than communing with the Lord, enjoying Christian fellowship, and being instructed from the Word. Some think it is good for business or enhances their social standing. Others make an appearance to display their piety. Some attend merely out of a sense of duty. Not one of these motives brings honor to God. But since we have our traditional sanctuary, our organ and our robed choirs, our priest or minister in his vestments, we can lay claim to "having a form of godliness, [though] denying its power" (2 Tim. 3:5).

Have we allowed our traditions and practices to obscure or even replace true worship? Do we believe that, as long as we show up for services and do the "right" kinds of things, we are worshiping—even if our hearts are filled with greed, lust, anger, and pride?

THINGS TO THINK ABOUT

1. How did the scribes come into existence? If they were sincere at first, why do you think they later fell into error?

2. To us, the tradition of *Corban* seems to be an obvious contradiction of the Law's intent. What do you think led the scribes to write such a law?

3. Read Isaiah 29. Why do you think Jesus decided to quote from this passage in confronting the Pharisees' hypocrisy?

4. The leaders were concerned about what goes *into* a man, and Jesus focused on what proceeds *out* of him. Describe the difference.

5. Is it possible today for our *outward* traditions of worship to hide our *inward* lack of heart for God? How can this phenomenon occur?

18

T R U E   W O R S H I P
I S   B A L A N C E D

*But the hour is coming, and now is, when the true worshipers
will worship the Father in spirit and truth; for the Father is
seeking such to worship Him.*

I n music, the standard for the note "A" is 440 vibrations per
second. A violin string that is too tight and vibrates too quickly,
or one that is too loose and vibrates too slowly, will not produce
an "A" regardless of the violinist's sincerity. Only the right amount of
tension produces a right sound.

Much of life consists of such tensions and balances. Balance is
critical, for example, even in such simple matters as eating, sleeping,
and exercise. Too much or too little of these things can undermine the
health of even the most robust man or woman.

A certain tension and balance is also God's standard for true
worship. The tendency of some Christians is a style of worship that is
strong on emotion. Others tend toward the opposite pole of worship
that is strongly based on intellect. Actually, the Bible makes it clear that
spirit and truth are both necessary for true worship. An overemphasis
on either spirit or truth will pervert our worship, rendering it a tribute
either to the flesh or to the intellect. Either aspect to the exclusion
of the other robs God of His glory. Those who worship God must
worship Him in spirit and in truth.

A biblical example of the proper tension, or balance, between spirit and truth is found in the account of Jesus' unlikely conversation with a Samaritan woman.

JESUS APPEALED TO THE SPIRIT

Jesus encountered this woman during a very busy time for Him, a time of much journeying. Jesus had recently begun His public ministry, going to the Jordan to be baptized by John, calling His first disciples, performing His first miracle at Cana, taking a brief sojourn in Capernaum, and then traveling down to Jerusalem where He cleansed the temple. Jesus was becoming known in Israel. Even one of the Jewish religious rulers sought a private audience with Jesus so that He could explain His teachings.

Then Jesus decided to return to Galilee. On the way there, He continued to do some very unconventional things. First of all, Jesus chose a route that most Jews would not have taken. Jesus set out on the most direct road from Jerusalem north to Galilee, a road most Jews would have strictly avoided. Instead, they would have headed due *east* to Jericho, crossed over to the *opposite* bank of the Jordan River, traveled north along the river valley, and then *re-crossed* the Jordan to enter Galilee. Why did they go so far out of the way? To avoid going through the land of Samaria.

What was so bad about Samaria? Northing more than the fact that it was where the Samaritans lived! And the Jews wanted nothing to do with the Samaritans. In their religious prejudice the Jews rejected the Samaritans' claim to be God's people also. The Jews maintained that they alone worshiped God correctly and that Samaritan worship practices were a perversion. For their part, the Samaritans returned the contempt and viewed the Jews as arrogant.

The Jews looked all the way back to Abraham as the father of their nation. God had personally called Abraham and given him a promise of which the Jews were the fulfillment. God had called their ancestors out of Egypt to become the nation of Israel and had given them the Law. When later they were disobedient, God permitted their captivity in Babylon. But after seventy years (in 530 B.C.), they returned to Jerusalem and rebuilt the city. Yes, the Jews were God's people.

But the Samaritans also claimed to be God's people. They, too, looked back to Abraham as their father. Their ancestors were the same people whom God called out of Egypt and to whom He gave His law. But the difference between the Jews and the Samaritans lay in the fact that the Samaritans' ancestors were the disobedient Jews of the ten northern tribes, the tribes who had split from the two southern tribes of Judah and Benjamin. God allowed the ten northern tribes, also, to be taken captive— but by the Assyrians in 622 B.C. When the Assyrians subjugated the region, they planted pagan Gentiles among the surviving Jews. The two groups intermarried to create the Samaritan nation. In the process, the former Jews were infected with the pagan worship of false gods.

Thus the Jews and Samaritans despised each other. But it was through Samaria that Jesus now journeyed on his way from Jerusalem to Galilee. Most unusual! Entering the city of Sychar and seeing a well, "Jesus therefore, being wearied with *His* journey, sat thus on the well" (John 4:6). It was strange enough for a Jew to be in a Samaritan city. But what followed was also quite unusual.

> A woman of Samaria came to draw water. Jesus said to her, "Give Me a drink." For His disciples had gone away into the city to buy food. Then the woman of Samaria said to Him, "How is it that You, being a Jew, ask a drink from me, a Samaritan woman?" For Jews have no dealings with Samaritans. (John 4:7-9)

Jews and Samaritans would never ask each other for a drink! Then, too, it was unusual for a man to ask a woman for a drink. In that day the sexes did not communicate openly as they do in our own culture. Women in that society were under the authority and protection of either father or husband. But Jesus removed the obstacle of prejudice by showing this Samaritan woman that there is no prejudice when it comes to God's wonderful gifts.

> Jesus answered and said to her, "If you knew the gift of God, and who it is who says to you, 'Give Me a drink,' you would have asked Him, and He would have given you living water." (John 4:10)

He freely offered the Samaritan woman the gift of salvation. How wonderful it is to know that the Lord does not withdraw His offer of salvation because you and I are not on the list of "approved" persons. And notice that, when Jesus makes the offer of salvation, He expects us to accept it. He said to the woman, "If you knew, you would take it!"

After finishing with the issue of prejudice, Jesus then removed the obstacle of pragmatism. Throughout the ages men have said, "I can't get saved now. What would people think? How would salvation affect me? And what about all the things I enjoy doing? I might have to give them up!" These are pragmatic barriers that people throw up to block their acceptance of Christ's free gift. For her part, the Samaritan woman also focused on a pragmatic, materialistic concern.

> The woman said to Him, "Sir, You have nothing to draw with, and the well is deep. Where then do You get that living water? Are You greater than our father Jacob, who gave us the well, and drank from it himself, as well as his sons and his livestock?" (John 4:11-12)

Like most people today, the Samaritan woman was so intent on the practical issues of life that she could not grasp what Jesus taught. No bucket meant no water! That conclusion seemed sensible. Further, the Samaritan woman cited her own religious heritage as an excuse for not accepting God's free gift. How familiar that excuse sounds! "I'm an American, and so I'm a Christian." "My father was a deacon." "I belong to a Christian denomination, so I must be okay. I don't need to be *saved.*"

Jesus went beyond the woman's material objections. He tried to take her understanding to another level by explaining the difference between mere water and His free gift of living water.

> Jesus answered and said to her, "Whoever drinks of this [literal] water will thirst again, but whoever drinks of the [spiritual] water that I shall give him will never thirst. But the water that I shall give him will become in him a fountain of water springing up into everlasting life." (John 4:13-14)

But the woman did not grasp what Jesus was driving at. "Sir, give me this water," she replied, "that I may not thirst, nor come here to draw" (4:15). Perhaps she was expressing a longing of her spirit, a desire of her innermost being. But there was no confession of sin, no receiving of the gift Christ offered her. The woman indicated that she did not want to be literally thirsty again, or make the long and arduous trip to and from the well. If she could avoid those things, she was all for this living water!

Like the Samaritan woman, we, too, may sense spiritual longings but attempt to satisfy them in the flesh. Satisfying spiritual desires in the flesh is the easy way, the way that seems to satisfy and costs us nothing. Many pastors and worship leaders struggle with the temptation to take the easy way. They know that people have a real desire for "something" in their spirits. But the temptation can be great to try to assuage the peoples' legitimate spiritual desires by feeding the impulses of the flesh, thereby gathering a crowd and building an organization.

Jesus wanted to guide the Samaritan woman beyond her limited material outlook to a higher level of real spiritual understanding. Today, pastors and churches that share that goal are not instantly popular. How much easier it is to give the masses what they want, to "bring them in" through appealing worship practices and hope you can later win them. But eventually, the people learn that the flesh is still unsatisfied and that the longing of the spirit is still with them.

JESUS APPEALED TO THE TRUTH

Once Jesus had explained His offer of salvation and the woman still did not understand, you would expect Jesus to try again. At least He had the woman's attention. She seemed open to learning more. Instead, Jesus took the conversation in an apparently abrupt and jarring direction: "Jesus said to her, 'Go, call your husband, and come here'" (John 4:16).

Where did *that* come from?

What Jesus intended in His command becomes more clear when we hear the woman's response. "The woman answered and said, 'I have no husband'" (4:17a). She wanted to maintain a facade of dignity so she did not immediately admit to Jesus that she had been engaged in multiple marriages and was currently living a degenerate lifestyle. She simply claimed that she had no husband, and her claim was true. However, her intent was to let Jesus believe she was a widow, a victim of desertion, or had never married; and none of these implications was true. Her claim was a facade.

Jesus had dealt earlier with the issues of prejudice and pragmatism, obstacles that could keep the Samaritan woman from accepting His gift of salvation. Now Jesus dealt with the obstacle of pride. None of us can receive Christ and truly worship Him until Jesus has torn away our facade—which is in reality a lie—and has helped us deal with our sin. Jesus knew the Samaritan woman needed to face the truth. For that reason, "Jesus said to her, 'You have well said, "I have no husband": For you have had five husbands; and the one whom you now have is not your husband: in that you spoke truly'" (4:17b-18).

Was Jesus unkind or tactless to expose the woman's sin and destroy her self-respect in such a direct manner? In fact, His statement was motivated by love. Once He removed her facade, Jesus and the Samaritan woman could begin to deal with truth on a level playing field. Similarly, you and I can never worship God in truth until His truth has been applied specifically to us and has uncovered our sins.

The Samaritan woman began at this point to understand that spiritual, not just physical issues were at stake. "The woman said to Him, 'Sir, I perceive that You are a prophet'" (4:19). Yet as soon as Jesus started talking about her sin, the woman did something that is still very common today. Seeing that the conversation had turned to "religion," she tried to shift the focus off her own failings. She was uncomfortable discussing her sin. So she switched the topic of conversation to the differences between various religions—in this case, the religions of the Jews and the Samaritans. "Our fathers worshiped on this mountain," the woman asserted, "and you Jews say that in Jerusalem is the place where one ought to worship" (4:20).

The religious tradition cited by the Samaritan woman dated to the time of Moses. As the Israelites prepared to enter the promised land, Moses commanded that "on the day when [they] cross over the Jordan" they should build an altar for God's glory (Deut. 27:2-8). Half of the people were to gather on Mount Ebal and the other half on Mount Gerizim, and in an antiphonal fashion the Israelites were to repeat the blessings and cursings of the law. As a result of this occasion, Mount Gerizim took on special meaning for the Samaritans. It became their traditional place of worship, standing in stark contrast to the temple worship of the Jews in Jerusalem. The Samaritan woman wanted to discuss that issue.

JESUS EXPLAINED THE RIGHT BALANCE

Such a response is typical when sinners are confronted with the truth about their sins. They try to shift the topic and talk about the differences among religions. But Jesus did not allow the woman to go far with the new topic. He turned her back to the real matter at hand, the matter of her salvation.

> Jesus said to her, "Woman, believe Me, the hour is coming when you will neither on this mountain, nor in Jerusalem, worship the Father. You worship what you do not know; we know what we worship, for salvation is of the Jews. But the hour is coming, and now is, when the true worshipers will worship the Father in spirit and truth; for the Father is seeking such to worship Him. God is Spirit, and those who worship Him must worship in spirit and truth." (John 4:21-24)

The Lord knew that in a couple of years He would pay the penalty for all sins on the cross. Because of this atonement, the traditional Jewish sacrificial system would no longer be needed. Temple worship would be voided. Jesus knew also that within a single generation, in A.D. 70, the Romans would destroy the temple. The present religious differences between the Jews and Samaritans would no longer matter.

In her traditional Samaritan worship at Mount Gerizim, the woman of Samaria thought she knew the truth. Now this woman began to realize that she might not. "The woman said to Him, 'I know that Messiah is coming (who is called Christ). When He comes, He will tell us all things'" (4:25). The Lord replied to her by establishing His authority to teach her about true worship. "Jesus said to her, 'I who speak to you am *He*'" (4:26). Jesus declared that He was the Messiah, the Christ.

And what was Jesus teaching her? In his conversation with the Samaritan woman, He had addressed her spiritual longing as well as her need for the truth. He had addressed the obstacles—prejudice and pragmatism, pride and tradition—that she raised. Now He told her that if she were to accept His free offer of salvation, her heart would become "a well of water springing up into everlasting life." Jesus said that this condition of the heart would naturally express itself through worship "in spirit and in truth."

Let us take a look at these two concepts, spirit and truth, one at a time. You and I must worship God in spirit because, as Jesus stated, "God is Spirit" (4:24). That truth means, among other things, that it is impossible to represent God by any material object. Icons and statues, religious art and stained glass windows—these do not fairly illustrate God. Nor can man relegate God to one place, even the most ornate cathedral or lavish church building. To worship God "in spirit" means, most importantly, that our worship must spring from within and flow from the heart. As we learned in the previous chapter, Jesus labeled as "vain" the worship of men who "draw near to Me with their mouth, and honor Me with their lips; but their heart is far from Me" (Matt. 15:8).

This concept reminds me of an illustration. When I was a boy, my mother sometimes made me go to the neighbor girls' birthday parties. That was the last thing I wanted to do on a Saturday! But I went anyway, ate the cake and ice cream, played the party games, and pretended to have a good time, all because my mother expected me to. For an eight-year-old boy, a girl's birthday party was a real drag. But when I was eighteen my attitude changed entirely! Now those neighborhood girls had turned into beautiful and talented young women. I loved to attend their parties because my heart was full of warm feelings toward them. It was natural for me to have a good time. Why did I now enjoy the parties? My attitude flowed from a sincere heart.

Worship follows the same principle. You and I must worship God from a sincere heart; we must not create a pretense of emotionalism that substitutes for real worship. Of course, since worship in the spirit flows from the heart—the seat of human emotion—true worship will engage our emotions. Yet it is possible for us to fake emotions (perhaps to fit in with the people around us) or to generate emotions (in response to those around us, or to those who know how to work an audience). Immature Christians often see emotion as the focus of worship. They try to be like "Paul and Silas [who] were praying and singing hymns to God" (Acts 16:25) despite being in prison. The unfeigned joy of Paul and Silas, however, sprang from the depths of their committed, faithful hearts.

Today we feel great pressure to skip the part about having a faithful heart. Our modern society has a "me first" attitude that seeks satisfaction without sacrifice. At the same time, our mass culture judges organizations by the numbers they generate. Putting the two phenomena together, we realize that the temptation is great for churches to draw crowds by playing to the emotions of the masses. The result is a cycle in which the people enjoy the worship experience but find their enjoyment short-lived, thus forcing worship leaders to be more creative. God does not expect us to worship that is without emotion, but He absolutely opposes worship without a right heart and a right spirit.

You and I must also worship God in truth. But what is truth? Does it correspond to your standard or mine? In fact, real truth is God's Word. Therefore Jesus prayed, "Sanctify them by Your truth: Your word is truth" (John 17:17). Only those who are conformed to God's standard—because they know His Word—can worship Him in truth. Sometimes that truth may be difficult, exposing our shame and sinfulness. But as Jesus made clear to the Samaritan woman, we must submit to His truth and remove the obstacles that keep us from His salvation and true worship.

It is possible for Christians to become so intent on the details of truth, however, that they forget to worship in spirit. We can become modern Pharisees, focused on intellectual musings about the letter of the law. In our evangelical subculture, for example, we sometimes know more about the teaching of a particular Christian author than we do about what God teaches in *His* book. Thus truth—even biblical truth—can be out of balance with spirit. The tension is not right, and like a violin string that is out of tune, we sound the wrong note.

An overemphasis on the intellectual pursuit of truth can kill our evangelistic zeal and cause us to become proud about what we know. Through such an overemphasis, we are in reality attempting to put the infinite God into our finite box of understanding. Worshiping in spirit and in truth—and with a biblical balance between the two—means that sometimes we will not be able to explain the infinite God!

Jesus taught us to keep the balance between spirit and truth. Both are essential for true worship. Overemphasis upon either leads to untrue worship. Although Jesus' disciples "marveled that He talked with the woman" of Samaria (John 4:27), we can be grateful that He conversed with her, and that God's Word records for us this very important lesson.

THINGS TO THINK ABOUT

1. Jesus offered salvation to a Samaritan. What does this fact say about *syncretism* (blending religions) and *universalism* (accepting all religions are okay) as means for societies to meet their spiritual needs?

2. What are some ways that people today try to satisfy their spiritual longings by feeding their flesh? Can Christians do this?

3. The Samaritan woman offered a *pragmatic* objection to what Jesus offered. What pragmatic objections do people give today?

4. Rather than face her sin and need for salvation, the woman tried to shift the conversation. Have you ever encountered a person who tried to do the same?

5. Explain in your own words the proper balance between spirit and truth in worship.

19

TRUE WORSHIP COMES BY KNOWING GOD

PAUL AND THE GREEKS • ACTS 17:16-34

Nor is [God] worshiped with men's hands, as though He needed any thing, since He gives to all life...that they should seek the Lord, in the hope that they might grope for Him and find Him.

Someone once told me that more than eight hundred churches are listed in our local phonebook. Among the Baptists alone there are Southern Baptists, American Baptists, National Baptists, Progressive National Baptists, Independent Baptists, Conservative Baptists, Regular Baptists, Reformed Baptists, Missionary Baptists, Free Will Baptists, Primitive Baptists, and even Seventh Day Baptists. And those are just the Baptists!

The listings in local phonebooks across the country also suggest the growing pluralism of American religious life. There are organizations that (either for the sake of convenience or for public acceptance) call themselves "churches" but worship nature, or ancestors, or idols carved by hands. And there are sincere people, even in my southern city, in the American South, who regularly bow before statues and pray.

All of these persons and organizations claim to be worshiping God. Who is right? Even if some are wrong, why should anyone try to change them? They claim to be happy and fulfilled by their faith.

The Bible makes clear, however, that God's people—people who are truly concerned about the true worship of God—should be provoked when they see idolatry. The Old Testament is rife with examples of this response to idolatry, from Elijah's slaying the prophets of Baal, to King Josiah's destroying the idol worship that had proliferated under his evil predecessors (2 Chron. 34:3-7; 2 Kings 23:4-20).

Similar crackdowns were instituted in the reigns of Asa (2 Chron. 14:2-3), Jehoshaphat (2 Chron. 17:6), and Hezekiah (2 Chron. 31:1; 1 Kings 18:5-6). Paul taught that Christians should learn from the examples of the Israelites. "Now all these things happened to them as examples, and they were written for our admonition" (1 Cor. 10:11). Consider these commands that God gave to the Israelites:

> But you shall destroy their altars, break their sacred pillars, and cut down their wooden images (for you shall worship no other god, for the LORD, whose name is Jealous, is a jealous God), lest you make a covenant with the inhabitants of the land, and they play the harlot with their gods and make sacrifice to their gods, and one of them invites you and you eat of his sacrifice. (Ex. 34:13-15)

> But thus you shall deal with them: you shall destroy their altars, and break down their sacred pillars, and cut down their wooden images, and burn their carved images with fire. For you are a holy people to the LORD your God; the LORD your God has chosen you to be a people for Himself, a special treasure above all the peoples on the face of the earth. (Deut. 7:5-6)

> And you shall destroy their altars, break their sacred pillars, and burn their wooden images with fire; you shall cut down the carved images of their gods and destroy their names from that place. (Deut. 12:3)

Responding To Idolatry

"But that was the Old Testament," you say. In the New Testament, however, we have the example of Paul, whose "spirit was provoked within him when he saw that the city was given to idols" (Acts 17:16). He was in Athens, the center of Greek culture. This was no primitive tribal idolatry he encountered, but that of a cosmopolitan civilization with a sophisticated culture—indeed, a civilization from which our own is descended. In other words, Paul found himself surrounded by a kind of idolatry that is familiar to us today.

And we do see it all around us! As Christians we are not called to go through life wearing blinders. God expects us to watch and observe what is happening around us. He especially desires that we be sensitive to spiritual conditions wherever we go. Paul certainly was observant in this way as he waited alone in Athens for his co-workers to arrive from Berea (Acts 17:13-15).

Paul was planning to return to Macedonia and continue the ministry to which God had called him. But as "Paul waited for them at Athens" (17:16) he was not idle. He walked the streets of the Greek capital and observed the spiritual needs of its people. Although Greece had long ceased to be a world power in its own right and had become a Roman province, Athens was still one of the leading cities in the empire and exerted a wide cultural influence. Centuries before, Athens had reached the height of political power under the leadership of Pericles. The Acropolis and the incomparable Parthenon had been constructed. Philip II of Macedon conquered the city in 338 B.C., but his son Alexander the Great spread Athenian culture throughout the known world. Then in 146 B.C. the Romans took the city. Skilled as they were in building and engineering, in matters of culture the Romans loved everything Greek. So Athens maintained a significant influence in the Roman world.

Athens was still a beautiful city in Paul's day, although it was smaller than it had been at its zenith. Some scholars estimate that the city had only ten thousand residents at this time. Paul would certainly have visited the lively city marketplace, called the *agora*. He would have observed the masterpieces of art and architecture, the temples and grand buildings with their opulent porches. He would have noted the many manifestations of human wisdom and philosophy. Learned debates continued in this former home of Plato, Aristotle, and Socrates.

Yet among all the sights and sounds of the city, Paul focused on its desperately lost spiritual condition. Idols and temples dedicated to a multitude of false gods abounded in Athens. In recording that Athens was "given over to idols" (Acts 17:16), the Bible uses a word meaning literally that the city was *smothered* by idolatry! Xenophon, a Greek historian and military leader gave the same account. He said, "Athens is one great altar, one great sacrifice. There are more gods in Athens than in all the rest of the country." Similarly, a Roman satirist joked that it was easier to find a god in Athens than to find a man.

Statues of ivory, silver, bronze, and gold fashioned by the most skillful Greek sculptors covered the landscape. Everywhere Paul looked he must have seen beautiful temples, shrines, and altars. Greatest of all was the Parthenon that housed the statue of Athena; the gleaming point of her spear could be seen forty miles away.

The Athens that Paul observed was much like the modern cities of America, which are likewise full of religious symbolism. We, too, live in a nation of great wealth, one of the leading nations of the world. One manifestation of our wealth is the beautiful and often ornate places of worship that can be seen in every American city. We proclaim ourselves to be a people of God by spending millions of dollars on our many temples and shrines.

Paul illustrates for us the believer's right response to such signs of false worship: "His spirit was provoked within him" (Acts 17:16). He was not a typical tourist, wandering the streets of Athens. He did not see his sojourn as a vacation from ministry. As Paul walked the Athenian streets and observed the idolatry, he was aroused to anger! That is the meaning of the Bible word translated "provoked." Paul did not lose his temper, but he became more and more indignant at what he saw. We, too, when we observe attempts to replace true worship of the true God, should be stirred in our spirits—stirred enough to do something!

From Paul's example we see that our first response to idolatry must be to proclaim the truth. "Therefore he reasoned in the synagogue with the Jews and with the *Gentile* worshipers, and in the marketplace daily with those who happened to be there" (17:17). Paul decided to begin evangelizing at the synagogue, to deal with Jews and the Gentile proselytes who had some grasp of the truth and claimed to be searching for God. Perhaps he could help them come to the knowledge of salvation as he reasoned with them. The word translated here as "reasoned" means that Paul argued with these people (in a positive sense) from the truths of their own scriptures.

Yet history reveals that, as a rule, these kinds of religious people rejected Paul's arguments. They responded much as do the many religious people in our own day who know much about what the Bible says but "reinterpret" portions that seem hard to accept. So we must explain to them such fundamental doctrines as the depravity of man, the virgin birth of Christ, His blood atonement, and the infallibility of the Bible. We must reason with such people in order to help them know salvation and become true worshipers of God.

But we must also speak to those who are ignorant of the true God. After he spoke in the synagogue, Paul went "in the marketplace daily" (17:17). The *agora* was a center of public life in Athens and was a logical place to find many opportunities for witnessing. Sure enough, it was there that Paul encountered "certain Epicurean and Stoic philosophers" (17:18).

REVEALING THE KNOWLEDGE OF GOD

The Epicureans were intellectual people who believed the world came together by chance. Since they believed they were not accountable to any Creator God, the Epicureans determined to enjoy life to the fullest. They taught that death is the end of everything, and that therefore people should strive to live without worry, pain, or discomfort. The Stoics had an opposite view. They believed in a supreme god, though they believed he might be manifested in many forms or in lesser gods. They taught that the course of all human life is determined by fate, and that people should learn to be self-sufficient and live in harmony with nature. The Stoics summed up the duty of man as submission to fate and learning to endure pain and discomfort.

We still deal with people like the Epicureans and Stoics, those who either "live for the moment" or "take whatever comes." Their lives are governed either by a constant quest for gratification, or by simply hoping somehow to muddle through the game of life. Based on his or her respective outlook, each type of individual would conclude, "What else could anyone do?" When you and I speak to them about Christ, therefore, we seem to be preaching a strange gospel. The Epicureans and Stoics certainly thought so.

> Then certain Epicurean and Stoic philosophers encountered him. And some said, "What does this babbler want to say?" Others said, "He seems to be a proclaimer of foreign gods," because he preached to them Jesus and the resurrection. (Acts 17:18)

These local philosophers took note of Paul for perhaps two reasons. First, as we learn from the biblical record, "all the Athenians and the foreigners who were there [in the *agora*] spent their time in nothing else, but either to tell or hear some new thing" (Acts 17:21). Another possible reason for their interest is that, as some scholars suggest, they might have misunderstood *Yesus* (Jesus) to be a god who had a female consort named *Anastasis*, Greek for resurrection. Although Rome was proud of her toleration of many gods, it was against the law to introduce new gods in a Roman city without the approval of the authorities. Thus,

> they took him and brought him to the Areopagus, saying, "May we know what this new doctrine is of which you speak? For you are bringing some strange things to our ears. Therefore we want to know what these things mean." (Acts 17:19-20)

Paul was not in a position to act as did the Israelite kings of old, to bring an army and cast down the pagan idols. But he showed true courage in testifying for his God before even the most influential Athenian authorities. The Areopagus was Athens's supreme court. Its name is derived from the location where this council met (translated "Mars Hill" in the King James Bible), until the court itself was called the Areopagus. Thus Paul had the privilege of speaking to the leaders who would decide whether he would be allowed to continue preaching Christ in Athens. When given this opportunity, the apostle boldly proclaimed the truths about God.

Then Paul stood in the midst of the Areopagus and said, "Men of Athens, I perceive that in all things you are very religious; for as I was passing through and considering the objects of your worship, I even found an altar with this inscription: to the unknown god. Therefore, the One whom you worship without knowing, Him I proclaim to you: God, who made the world and everything in it, since He is Lord of heaven and earth, does not dwell in temples made with hands. Nor is He worshiped with men's hands, as though He needed anything, since He gives to all life, breath, and all things. And He has made from one blood every nation of men to dwell on all the face of the earth, and has determined their preappointed times and the boundaries of their dwellings." (Acts 17:22-26)

These were bold words indeed! Paul told the court that its religious devotions were "superstitious" and "ignorant." His hearers were the most important authorities in the city, men who could put him in prison. At first, Paul acknowledged that they were very religious. The court may have thought this acknowledgement was a compliment—until they heard the rest of what the apostle had to say. Paul was in a difficult circumstance, but he did not flinch from giving the truth. Sometimes we, too, have the chance to speak with people who are religious but wrong. What do we say to them? Are we bold as Paul was?

Although the apostle did not mince words, neither did he engage in *ad hominem* argument. Paul made his case by drawing clear lines of distinction between truth and error. In so doing, he proclaimed four basic truths: that God is the only known and true God; that He is Creator both of the world and of every man; that the Author of life cannot be put into the box of man's religious theories; and that, because God determines man's boundaries in life, He is, therefore, the eternal Judge of every person.

Religious people often err in their worship by denying these four basic truths. They presume to know and worship God but seldom study the biblical revelation of Him very seriously. They may say God is the Creator, but they act as though they are not subject to Him. They say He is the supreme authority, but in their doctrines they refuse to consider God to be infinite. They claim that God is omnipotent but they do not trust Him to draw the boundaries of their lives. Therefore, they really do not believe that God is the eternal Judge to whom they are accountable. In contrast to their beliefs, Paul proclaimed that all people are responsible before God to "seek the Lord, in the hope that they might grope for Him and find Him, though He is not far from each one of us; for in Him we live and move and have our being, as also some of your own poets have said, 'For we are also His offspring'" (Acts 17:27-28).

Paul was not arguing that people must seek God through their own experiences. That path leads only to the confusing maze of man's finite existence. Granted, some searchers have used their God-given intellects to come very *near* the truth. Paul acknowledged as much by quoting the Greek poet Aratus. Yet ultimately, all men who seek God apart from His divine revelation in the Scriptures get stuck in the quagmire of human error. We must challenge all people to seek Him in the Scriptures, for it is in the Scriptures that He has revealed Himself.

No, seeking the Lord is not a matter of human wisdom or experience. As Paul went on to explain, we dare not seek Him through the idolatrous creations of our own hands. Rather, we must seek Him by repenting from sin and throwing ourselves upon the mercies of God. In his defense before the Areopagus, Paul taught that men must seek the Lord in light of His coming judgment, which will be based on each person's relationship with Jesus Christ.

> Therefore, since we are the offspring of God, we ought not to think that the Divine Nature is like gold or silver or stone, something shaped by art and man's devising. Truly, these times of ignorance God overlooked, but now commands all men everywhere to repent, because He has appointed a day on which He will judge the world in righteousness by the Man whom He has ordained. He has given assurance of this to all by raising Him from the dead. (Acts 17:29-31)

You and I must, like Paul, remind people to search for the true God because someday He will call every man to account. This is our responsibility, to proclaim the truth of the Word—even if, as they were for Paul, the results seem meager. Paul declared the truth, and his testimony was heard by thinking people and religious seekers in the synagogue, the marketplace, and the city hall. Many were confronted with the truth about God, but few yielded. "And when they heard of the resurrection of the dead, some mocked, while others said, 'We will hear you again of this matter'" (17:32). In other words, some men scoffed, and others put Paul off.

"So Paul departed from among them" (17:33). When the people made their choices to reject truth, they also forfeited the work of truth in their lives. These men opted to leave the truth, and so Paul, the teacher of truth, left them. They made a deadly decision.

The great news, however, is that "some men joined him and believed" (17:34). The Bible records that these converts included a member of the Areopagus, one woman, and "others with them." They turned from the false worship of an unknown god to the true worship of the true God. The fact that only a few people accepted the truth does not mean Paul failed. Nor does it mean that the truth failed. The truth cannot fail! This reality is as valid today as it was in the time of Paul. When we tell of Christ, perhaps only a few will trust Him. But that result is still a glorious success, for every person who yields to God's truth is an eternal trophy of His grace.

Idolatry and false worship are all around us. How are you responding to the idolatry in your own Athens? Does it stir your spirit to make known the truths of God?

Things to Think About

1. Paul was sensitive to the idolatry around him. What idolatry do you see today that "stirs" your spirit?

2. What was Paul's initial response to the idolatry he saw? How could you apply that same response in your circumstances?

3. How do the Epicureans and Stoics remind you of people you encounter today? Are their objections to Christ similar?

4. In your own words, summarize Paul's line of argument before the Athenian court.

5. Human wisdom can come near the truth, as did that of the Greek poet. Can you think of examples of such human wisdom today? Why does it fall short?

20

TRUE WORSHIP
BOASTS IN CHRIST
ALONE

For we are the circumcision, who worship God in the Spirit,
rejoice in Christ Jesus, and have no confidence in the flesh.

Howard Rutledge, a United States Air Force pilot, was shot down over North Vietnam during the Vietnam War. He survived, and spent several years in a POW camp before his release at the war's conclusion. Recalling his time in the "Heartbreak Hotel," Rutledge wrote how his view of life was changed by his loss of temporal treasures.

> During those longer periods of enforced reflection it became so much easier to separate the important from the trivial, the worthwhile from the waste. For example, in the past, I usually worked or played hard on Sundays and had no time for church.... But in Heartbreak solitary confinement, there was no pastor, no Sunday School teacher, no Bible, no hymnbook, no community of believers to guide and sustain me. I had completely neglected the spiritual dimension of my life. It took prison to show me how empty life is without God.

Throughout the history of our nation's wars, many soldiers have come home from captivity to share similar stories. In more recent history, Christian workers held prisoner by terrorists have testified that their experiences made God real to them. Remembering her imprisonment under Afghanistan's Taliban regime, Heather Mercer later recounted how her circumstances prompted a true surrender to God: "I ceased putting my hope in the end result of our crisis. My hope rested in the promise I had for eternity. Whether my natural life ended in prison or not, I knew I would live forever in heaven with Jesus. Though the Taliban could imprison my body, they could no longer imprison my spirit."

Nearly two millenia ago, another missionary held in captivity related what he had learned. "I count all things loss," wrote the apostle Paul, "for the excellence of the knowledge of Christ Jesus my Lord, for whom I have suffered the loss of all things, and count them as rubbish, that I may gain Christ" (Phil. 3:8). In reality, every Christian should identify with the radical change in values that takes place as a result of our own "prison" experience.

> Even so we, when we were [spiritual] children, were in bondage
> under the elements of the world. But when the fullness of the time
> had come, God sent forth His Son, born of a woman, born under
> the law, to redeem those who were under the law, that we might
> receive the adoption as sons. And because you are sons, God has
> sent forth the Spirit of His Son into your hearts, crying out, "Abba,
> Father!" Therefore you are no longer a slave but a son, and if a
> son, then an heir of God through Christ....Stand fast therefore
> in the liberty by which Christ has made us free, and do not be
> entangled again with a yoke of bondage. (Gal. 4:3-7, 5:1)

When you and I begin to comprehend all that Christ is to us, like Paul we count "all things loss" in comparison. That attitude will become the foundation of our worship to the Lord, the natural expression of hearts into which "God has sent forth the Spirit of His Son."

T RUE W ORSHIP D RAWS D ISTINCTIONS

Paul opens his heart to the Philippians, beginning this section of his letter with a good-news-bad-news statement. First comes the good news: "Finally, my brethren, rejoice in the Lord" (3:1). You and I, if we know Christ, have every reason to be joyful! Indeed, we are without excuse if our worship does not reflect our joy in Him.

In admonishing the Philippian believers to rejoice, Paul was fully aware that Jesus said, "If they persecuted me, they will also persecute you" (John 15:20). Who better than Paul would understand this truth? As a Pharisee he had once "breath[ed] threats and murder against the disciples of the Lord" (Acts 9:1). Now, following his conversion, he had "suffered the loss of all things." Yet Paul could proclaim with the greatest of all joy "that Christ Jesus came into the world to save sinners, of whom I am chief" (1 Tim. 1:15). True rejoicing is rooted in the Lord and flows from a sincere appreciation for salvation from sin's penalty and power.

Abruptly, however, Paul switches gears and gives the bad news. Even when we read Paul's letter today, the shift is jarring. Paul, who founded the Philippian church about a decade earlier, had communicated with the believers on this matter before: "To write the same things to you, *is* not tedious, but for you *it is* safe" (Phil. 3:1). And what was this matter?

> Beware of dogs, beware of evil workers, beware of the mutilation.
> (Phil. 3:2)

Dogs? What did Paul mean? The apostle was addressing the problem of hypocritical service to God—specifically, three traits of a hypocritical Jewish group that plagued the early church.

First, Paul characterized these hypocrites as "dogs." His readers would have immediately understood Paul's reference to dogs. Today we think of dogs as furry pets or loyal companions. But in biblical times most dogs were wild and ran in packs. They barked at strangers and bit people. They fought among themselves, ate refuse and filth, and carried disease. Peter once quoted "the true proverb: A dog returns to his own vomit" (2 Peter 2:22).

The Gentile believers at Philippi would have understood a not-so-subtle irony in Paul's words. Jews were famous in the ancient world for referring to all Gentiles as dogs. But men called "Judaizers" had been following Paul all around Asia, disrupting the new churches and sowing confusion among believers. They claimed to be Christians but insisted that believers must follow the Mosaic law to obtain full salvation. So in warning the Philippians to "beware of dogs," Paul was turning the Judaizers' own insult back upon themselves. For these false teachers were spiritually unclean, ravening and contemptible, roaming in packs, and stirring up trouble like quarreling dogs.

Second, Paul called the Judaizers "evil workers." They were zealous and relentless in pressing their interpretation. Even after the church council in Jerusalem had warned against applying Mosaic law to new believers (Acts 15:1-31), the Judaizers persisted. They were workers indeed, but evil workers. These men appeared to be very religious, in their outward deportment perhaps even more religious than Paul was. But in reality, these workers were malicious, deceitful religionists who lived in sin and promoted sin against God.

Third, Paul warned the church to "beware of the mutilation." In effect, the apostle was saying that the Judaizers were mutilated. What did he mean? These false teachers gloried in the ordinance of circumcision. To them, it was the greatest external act of religion that one could perform. The Judaizers concluded that the ceremony of circumcision was the distinguishing difference between redeemed people and perishing people. But the problem with the Judaizers was that their hearts were not circumcised. They meticulously kept up religious externals; but those externals are not what God desires among His people.

"Therefore circumcise the foreskin of your heart," the Lord declared, "and be stiff-necked no longer" (Deut. 10:16). Moses also promised Israel, "And the LORD your God will circumcise your heart, and the heart of your descendants, to love the LORD your God with all your heart, and with all your soul, that you may live" (Deut. 30:6). Paul himself summed up the LORD's true intent for His people: "In Him you were also circumcised with the circumcision made without hands, by putting off the body of the sins of the flesh, by the circumcision of Christ" (Col. 2:11).

In issuing his warning about the Judaizers, Paul did not find it tedious to "write of the same things" repeatedly. Neither should we, for religionists like the Judaizers are still among us. They downplay the simple gospel. They quarrel and fight, relentlessly push their agenda, and yet focus on nonessential issues. Often they insist that theirs is the only true standard of righteousness. In our day, some religionists may debate a religious ritual. Others may seek to intellectualize the clear teachings of God's Word. Still others insist that the gospel is not enough, that the church needs human methods and wisdom to supplement the Scriptures and attract the masses. To the Judaizers and to their kind now as then, Paul draws a stark contrast:

> For we are the circumcision, who worship God in the Spirit, rejoice
> in Christ Jesus, and have no confidence in the flesh. (Phil. 3:3)

How does Paul choose to illustrate the difference between the false teachers and the true believers? By their worship!

In telling the Philippians, "we are the circumcision," Paul did not intend to be arrogant or proud. By continuing the thought of circumcision, Paul was communicating the truth that true believers have the sin and impurity removed from their hearts. Only those with circumcised hearts can give God true worship. Christians need not be ashamed to draw this kind of distinction between the false and the genuine. Is it wrong to boast about the work God did in your heart? Of course not. You and I did not circumcise our own hearts; God Himself performed this special work, "the circumcision made without hands."

Paul lists key characteristics of true worship, worship that comes from a circumcised heart. First, such worship is offered in the Holy Spirit. True worshipers do not try to glorify God through the inventions of their minds, to "create" worship through impressive ritual pageantry or the arts of audience manipulation.

Second, true worshipers "rejoice in Christ Jesus" and not in their personal accomplishments or achieved emotional state. We rejoice in the person and work of Christ! If a church is full of people who know little about Christ and His work, how can a true worship service take place? How can the congregation rejoice in One, of whom they know so little? Since true worship rejoices in Christ, we can easily conclude that a worship service should seek to make Christ better known through the exposition of the Word. At one church you may encounter honored traditions and rituals that make the people feel secure. At another church, you may hear inspirational stories and music that makes the congregation feel warm and happy. Often these worship methods can attract a crowd; in fact, they do every Sunday all across our land. But without the Word of God to make Christ known, is true worship taking place?

Third, Paul stated that true worshipers "have no confidence in the flesh." There should be no place in our worship for boasting in our own efforts. Instead we revel and rejoice in the clear working of God, in our lives and in the lives of others, to make us more like the Christ we love.

TRUE WORSHIP COUNTS CHRIST

The Judaizers gloried in religious appearances and fleshly externals. If he had desired to do so, Paul could easily have beaten them at their own game! "I also might have confidence in the flesh," he wrote. "If anyone else thinks that he may have confidence in the flesh, I more so" (Phil. 3:4). As Paul went on to relate, he was "circumcised the eighth day, of the stock of Israel, of the tribe of Benjamin, a Hebrew of the Hebrews; concerning the law, a Pharisee; concerning zeal, persecuting the church; concerning the righteousness which is in the law, blameless" (Phil. 3:5-6).

Since he was circumcised at birth, Paul would have been deemed better than those Jews who were adult converts. He could trace his lineage through Benjamin back to Jacob, the man to whom God had given the name Israel, "for you have struggled with God and with men, and have prevailed" (Gen. 32:28). Paul's ancestry was highly significant. Whereas the Ishmaelites were related to Abraham through Hagar, and the Edomites were related to Isaac through Esau, only the pure Jews, God's people, were related to Israel. Paul could boast of being born of the tribe of Benjamin, furthermore, the tribe most faithful to God.

Before his conversion Paul had been one of the Pharisees, the strictest sect among the Jews. He was set so zealously against cults that opposed "true religion" that he consented to the death of Christians. In every way, he had been blameless according to the Judaizers' own religious standards. "But" Paul concluded, "what things were gain to me, these I have counted loss for Christ" (Phil. 3:7).

True worship places supreme value in Christ. This supreme regard for Christ requires us to take a proper view of our human gains and achievements. Do they help or hinder our worship? You and I must be honest with ourselves! We would do well to follow the advice of Hudson Taylor, the great missionary-statesman of China. "Let us give up our work," he urged, "our plans, ourselves, our lives, our loved ones, our influence, our all, right into God's hand; and then, when we have given all to Him, there will be nothing left for us to be troubled about."

Why must we give up our human gains "into God's hand"? Because a proper view of our worldly gains, a view that "counts all things but loss," contributes to a proper assessment of the value of Christ. Nothing in our lives is more valuable than He is. Nothing else in the world means more than our relationship with our Savior. When we value Christ above all else, our worship will evidence that fact. You and I will not need to invent ways to feel worshipful. True worship will flow naturally from a dedicated heart, a heart guided by the Holy Spirit so that God alone receives the glory.

THINGS TO THINK ABOUT

1. What attitude needs to be the foundation of our worship of the Lord Jesus Christ?

2. According to Philippians 3:2, what three traits plagued the early Church?

3. How did Paul illustrate the difference between the false teachers and the true teachers?

4. What are the three characteristics of true worship that stem from a circumcised heart?

5. How well does Hudson Taylor's statement about sacrificial service characterize your worship?

PART 4

THE CONTENT OF
TRUE WORSHIP

TRUE WORSHIP GLORIFIES GOD

Therefore, whether you eat or drink, or whatever you do, do all to the glory of God.

O nce I ran over a piece of metal on the highway. Instantly my gas tank was punctured and its entire contents dumped on the pavement. When I explained the mishap to a friend who knows about cars, he replied, "You're lucky that you weren't knocking on the gates of glory."

Glory is a word that is very common in American culture. It evokes feelings of pride and of excellence. We pledge allegiance to "Old Glory." Most children learn to sing, "Glory, glory, hallelujah!" from the *Battle Hymn of the Republic*. We routinely speak of heroic athletes who, giving their last ounce of strength, are striving for glory.

What does *glory* really mean? It is a flag fluttering in the breeze? A victory in battle? Heroism in athletic competition?

Surely the word must mean something more. Flags and battles and athletics are all normal affairs of human society. To be truly glorious, a thing must transcend the normal. But our casual use of the word pulls the concept of *glory* from its lofty meaning and places it in an ordinary setting.

Glory is something special, and God's glory is infinitely more special. God's glory is of supreme importance to Him. It is the reason

He created this world and all of us who populate it. You and I exist to manifest, to affirm and to exalt God's glory. As author John Piper puts it, God's pursuit of glory is "the invincible end for which He created the world." He created it so "that the glory of God might be magnified in the universe…that Christ's ransomed people from all times and all nations would rejoice in God above all things."

Because we overuse the word most Americans have trouble grasping the real truth regarding God's glory. As we focus on the Scripture passages that describe God's glory and His purpose in creation, however, we realize that most Christians, also, are deficient in understanding what the Bible says about this crucial concept.

GOD'S GLORY IS OUR PURPOSE

It is one thing to *say* that God's glory is our purpose in life, but it is quite a different thing to *understand* the statement we have just made. What *is* God's glory? God's glory can be briefly defined as His awesome supremacy and divine mode of being. Yet because God is the everlasting, self-existing, Almighty Creator, His full glory must escape our complete comprehension. He is infinite, but we are not.

In fact, God's glory is so immense that it would be deadly for us to see its fullness. Moses asked the LORD, "Please, show me Your glory" (Ex. 33:18). God agreed to "make all My goodness pass before you" and to "proclaim the name of the LORD before you," but He warned Moses, "You cannot see My face: for no man shall see Me and live" (33:19-20). God could reveal only small portions of His glory to His creation.

All that you and I will ever see of God's glory are limited manifestations of His overwhelming divinity. Yet even as the Lord answered Moses' request to see Him better, He grants us, too, such a privilege. In the Bible we read scores of accounts in which God reveals His glory through His mighty works: the Creation, the Flood, the Tower of Babel, the Exodus, the Conquest. It is no wonder that David, recalling such awesome displays of love and might, wrote,

Yours, O LORD, is the greatness, the power and the glory, the victory and the majesty; for all that is in heaven and in earth is

Yours; Yours is the kingdom, O LORD, and You are exalted as head over all. (1 Chron. 29:11)

The classical Greek word from which we derive our English word *glory* denotes an opinion. We, as God's created beings, should have a right opinion about God. This concept of glory is evident often in the Old Testament as the Israelites revere Yahweh (or fail to revere him) in recognition for what He had done.

In the New Testament, however, the concept of glory as an "opinion" regarding God's past works is completely superseded. *Glory* becomes in the New Testament a term to convey recognition of His intrinsic divinity. We read that God is "worthy...to receive glory and honor and power: for You have created all things, and by Your will they exist and were created" (Rev. 4:11). Since God intends for all His creation to glorify Him, glorifying Him should be the burning desire of those who claim to be His people. "Everyone who is called by My name, whom I have created for My glory; I have formed him, yes I have made him" (Is. 43:7).

But you and I cannot honor what we do not know. Let me suggest an illustration. Over the past generation, observance of Memorial Day has fallen into disuse. At one time the holiday fell on the last day of May. Now as a cost saving measure, it simply falls on the last Monday in May, so that federal workers will confine their long weekends to only three days. Our parents and grandparents can remember when Memorial Day was a solemn occasion for stately military parades and special church services, a day when families would put flowers on the graves of their fallen soldiers. Today, however, our education system often disdains nationalism. Students graduate from school with little understanding of American history or the sacrifices made to preserve our freedoms. Almost universally, Memorial Day is observed today merely as the official start of summer, a day to fire up the grill and break out the picnic baskets.

In short, on Memorial Day people give glory to themselves. We do not give honor to past heroes, simply because we simply do not know of their deeds. We cannot honor them if we do not know of them. In the same way, we cannot honor God's glory if we do not know that glory. But *how* can we know His glory? It is not true that mere men cannot fully know God's glory? Yes, that is true. But as we noted before, God gave Moses a glimpse of His glory. We have the same privilege; in fact, we are privileged to see some manifestations of glory that Moses never knew.

God reveals His glory, first, through His creation. The heavens "declare the glory of God" and "declare His righteousness, and all the peoples see His glory" (Ps. 19:1, 97:6). In the New Testament we read that "since the creation of the world, His invisible attributes are clearly seen, being understood by the things that are made, even his eternal power and Godhead; so that they [unbelievers] are without excuse" (Rom. 1:20). God's majesty is evident all around us, but we must pay attention to it in order to see it.

Second, God has chosen on occasion to reveal His glory through miraculous circumstances. Such miracles were greatly in evidence during the time of Moses and then the settling of the Promised Land. God's glory was evident again during the ministry of the prophets, when Israel was in rebellion against God. During the Babylonian captivity, God revealed His glory by working miraculously in the lives of Daniel and his three companions. And, of course, the greatest display of God's glory is the ministry of Christ, which led to the founding of the Church.

Besides revealing His glory through miracles and creation, God reveals His glory in the Bible. He does so not only in the many accounts of His miracles. God has given us all that we need in order to know Him.

> His divine power has given to us all things that pertain to life and godliness, through the knowledge of Him who called us by glory and virtue, by which have been given to us exceedingly great and precious promises, that through these you may be partakers of the divine nature, having escaped the corruption that is in the world through lust. (2 Pet. 1:2-4)

Finally, God reveals His glory in the hearts of those of His people who are tender and sensitive to hear Him. Paul expressed this truth when he expressed his desire "that I may know Him, and the power of His resurrection, and the fellowship of His sufferings, being conformed to His death" (Phil. 3:10). The Greek word that is translated "know" means to learn through intimate experience. A person first *believes* God in his heart, then *learns* of God in his heart, and at last comes to *know* God in his heart. When that happens, when you and I know God intimately, we can truly honor His glory.

You have probably had the experience of talking to someone who is passionate about his favorite pastime. Maybe this person's hobby is computers; he can talk about megabytes and gigabytes until his conversation begins to seem like a foreign language. Perhaps he is a sports fan who knows everything about his team, including individual stats, player incomes, and recent trades and signings. We glorify the things we know best—and we know best the things with which we spend the most time.

GOD'S GLORY IS OUR GOAL

Glorifying God rather than self runs counter to human nature. Why? Because you and I are innately selfish.

Our selfishness started with Satan's sin. "How you are fallen from heaven, O Lucifer....For you have said in your heart, I will ascend into heaven, I will exalt my throne above the stars of God;...I will be like the most High" (Is. 14:12-14). "Your heart was lifted up because of your beauty; you corrupted your wisdom for the sake of your splendor" (Ezek. 28:17). Satan became dissatisfied with the position God gave him and determined to gain more glory for himself. He fell because of selfishness.

This same Satan later infected humanity with his corruption. Hearkening to his lies, Eve "saw that the tree was good for food, that it was pleasant to the eyes, and a tree desirable to make one wise[.] [S]he took of its fruit, and ate. She also gave to her husband with her and he ate" (Gen. 3:6). Eve, like Satan who tempted her, did not trust that God knew what was best for her. She desired something that seemed better than His provision and concluded that her own selfish desires were paramount. She was more concerned about her perceived needs than she was about lifting up God's glory.

Thus sin entered the world, with the result that selfishness is obvious in all men. "There is none righteous, no, not one: There is none who understands, there is none who seeks after God. They have all turned aside; they have together become unprofitable; there is none who does good, no, not one" (Rom. 3:10-12). We seek our own glory because, in our natural state, "There is no fear of God before [our] eyes" (Rom. 3:18).

So it is little wonder that, when we go to worship, we manifest our innate selfishness. Today, for example, it is typical for a local paper to note that a musician is *performing* at a given church. After the musician sings, applause is common. Perhaps the applause is a spontaneous expression that joins the musician in giving glory to God. But let us be completely honest with ourselves. Has applause really become more a matter of accepted church etiquette or of honoring the musician?

What the modern world of religion calls "worship" can be a means to selfish ends. We have all heard stories about preachers who structure their services to attract an audience, collect money, build a big ministry, and then make a name for themselves. Often, lost men and women cite such stories out of all proportion to indict Christianity and justify their rejection of the gospel. Of course, the vast majority of preachers are sincere. But tragically, instances of empire building can and do exist within the ministry.

Perhaps even more troubling is the way that even faithful pastors can be swayed by the spirit of the age. How easy it is to schedule certain evangelists or music groups, in part because they will "draw a crowd." The rationalization is that when we get a crowd to come out to church, we can preach the gospel and bring the lost into the Kingdom. But even such seemingly righteous reasoning is flawed; it is God's work to save souls. If we try to save souls by our own methods, we act in selfishness to rob God of His deserved glory!

Our worship must focus on God's glory and lift it up for all to see. Jonathan Edwards, the great eighteenth-century American theologian, observed that, "true saints have their minds, in the first place, inexpressibly pleased and delighted with…the things of God." By contrast, he noted, hypocrites "first rejoice…that they are made so much of by God; and then on that ground, He seems in a sort, lovely to them."

Glorifying God is something we *do*, for the Word of God commands us to "do all to the glory of God" (1 Cor. 10:31). In other words, whatever we *do* we must *do* for God's glory. Therefore, glorifying God is a matter of obedient submission.

Obedience is formed first in the heart. It is in the heart that we believe God, that we purpose to know God from His Word, and that we determine to obey what we learn. Submission is a response to God's work in our lives for His own glory. "For it is God who works in you both to will and to do for His good pleasure" (Phil. 2:13). God teaches, convicts, and moves us by the principles of His Word. Then you and I must yield to the Holy Spirit as He works out those truths in our hearts.

Our submission to "do all to the glory of God" will be reflected in our worship. We will meet with other believers to join in singing about, praying about, and preaching about God's glory. Our minds and hearts will be filled with exuberance as we reflect on God's greatness and exalt the One we love. Such worship will challenge men and women in the world as we reveal to them the glorified God. True worshipers will say,

> Oh, give thanks to the LORD! Call upon His name; make known His deeds among the peoples! Sing to Him, sing psalms to Him; talk of all His wondrous works! Glory in His holy name; let the hearts of those rejoice who seek the Lord! Seek the Lord and His strength; seek His face evermore! Remember His marvelous works which He has done, His wonders, and the judgments of His mouth. (1 Chron. 16:8-12)

THINGS TO THINK ABOUT

1. What is the difference between *glory* as an "opinion" and *glory* as an intrinsic quality?

2. Moses had a glimpse of God's glory. What are four ways that we also can learn more about His glory?

3. Why is it that humans are innately selfish and seek their own glory? What was the root cause of our selfishness? How did it spread to all mankind?

4. Selfishness can manifest itself when we go to worship. Why is it so easy to enter worship with an attitude that is not focused on God?

5. "Do all to the glory of God." Explain in your own words why glorifying God is a matter of obedient submission.

TRUE WORSHIP EXPRESSES GREAT FAITH

JACOB • HEBREWS 11:21

By faith Jacob, when he was dying, blessed each of the sons of Joseph, and worshiped, leaning on the top of his staff.

After September 11, 2001, the thought of being in a doomed aircraft became all too real to contemplate. On that horrific day all America was grieved by stories of men and women who called loved ones for a final farewell. Yet amidst the awful devastation, an entire nation took heart from the heroism of Todd Beamer. "Let's roll!" he urged his fellow passengers, leading them in a charge against the terrorists who had hijacked their plane. His action saved possibly hundreds of lives on the ground, though he and all others aboard the airplane were lost when it crashed in a remote area.

Experts who investigate air disasters have long known that flight recordings can reveal a wide range of human emotion. When the black box is recovered and the recording analyzed, voices from the last moments before impact are often heard shouting vile and profane curses against God and fate. Other voices, however, pray to that same God for deliverance, whether in this life or the next.

How would you react in a similar situation? How would I react? Although the scenario is almost too horrible to consider, the answer would say much about our relationship with God. It would say much about how we lived our lives in the years preceding our end. Of course, if the Lord tarries in His coming, you and I will both face physical death someday. It may come in a traffic intersection, on an operating table, or in our own bed. But the day of our death will come. How will we meet it? What will our last actions and words say about us?

Jacob worshiped God through faith, even with his last breath. His worship was true and consistent. When the New Testament writer to the Hebrews was inspired by God to write the chapter we call the "Hall of Faith," he penned just one verse to illustrate the faith of Jacob. Fittingly, he chose an example from the patriarch's last days, when Jacob by faith "blessed both the sons of Joseph; and worshiped" (Heb. 11:21).

Why was this action significant? Why did it demonstrate such faith that, alone among all the deeds of Jacob, this final action is cited by the writer to the Hebrews? Read on.

JACOB ACTED BY FAITH

Ironically, this honored member of the "Hall of Faith" bears a name that actually means "supplanter." The name Jacob literally means "heel catcher," and it describes someone who will snatch you down by the heel if you are not alert. Sadly, Jacob spent most of his years living up to his name and practicing many deceptions. Yet the Lord later changed his name to Israel (Gen. 32:28), which means "God prevails." God made the name change after a long process that brought Jacob to a deep trust in Him.

Given the importance of Jacob's new name, it seems odd that the Word of God, as conveyed by the writer to the Hebrews, would list Jacob in the Hall of Faith under his old name. Perhaps this name is a reminder of God's great work of sanctification in Jacob's life. Thus Jacob serves as an Old Testament example of the same sanctification God wants us to experience today. You and I would do well, when we enter into worship, to remember how far God has brought us since the time we placed our trust in Him for salvation. Maybe Jacob was remembering the same thing as he lay dying; perhaps those thoughts were the cause of his worship.

Indeed, Jacob had much to think about as he recalled the 147 years of his life (Gen. 47:29). In his first fifty years, Jacob's life was characterized by sinful scheming. During the next eighty years he reaped the evil he had sown. No wonder, then, that when Pharaoh asked Jacob, "How old are you?" the patriarch replied, "The days of the years of my pilgrimage are one hundred and thirty years: few and evil have been the days of the years of my life" (47:8-9). At that time, seventeen years before his death, Jacob still had trouble remembering how God had forgiven and blessed him.

As a youth, Jacob deceived his father Isaac and sinned against his brother Esau by taking Esau's birthright. Because of his deed, Jacob was forced to leave his family and flee to a foreign land (Gen. 27:41-28:5). Yet even then, God was working to bring Jacob into a trusting relationship with Himself. Even as Jacob left home, the Lord provided guidance and encouragement through the counsel of his father Isaac. He blessed his son, urged him not to take a heathen wife, and advised Jacob where he should go: "Arise, go to Padanaram...and take yourself a wife from there of the daughters of Laban your mother's brother." Then, as father and son parted, Isaac declared,

> May God Almighty bless you, and make you fruitful and multiply you, that you may be an assembly of peoples; and give you the blessing of Abraham, to you and your descendants with you, that you may inherit the land in which you are a stranger, which God gave to Abraham. (Gen. 28:3-4)

During Jacob's journey, God met him in a dream. The Lord not only confirmed the blessing Isaac had given, but made Jacob an unconditional promise:

> The land on which you lie I will give to you and your descendants. Also your descendants...shall spread abroad...and in you and in your seed all the families of the earth shall be blessed. Behold, I am with you and will keep you wherever you go, and will bring

you back to this land; for I will not leave you until I have done what I have spoken to you. (Gen. 28:13-15)

Jacob did not throw himself on God's mercy when he heard this promise. But his response to the dream indicates that he was thinking seriously about his relationship with God. "Surely the Lord is in this place; and I did not know it," Jacob exclaimed when he awoke. He then piled some stones into an altar, poured oil upon it, and called the place Bethel, which means "house of God." Yet Jacob did not trust God completely to provide for His needs, and he continued to put God to the test.

> Then Jacob made a vow, saying, "If God will be with me...so that I come back to my father's house in peace, then the Lord shall be my God. And this stone which I have set as a pillar shall be God's house, and of all that You give me I will surely give a tenth to You." (Gen. 28:20-22)

After Jacob arrived at his destination, God provided him a wife—although ironically, Jacob obtained *two* wives after enduring the trickery of his uncle (Gen. 29). In the years he lived with Laban, Jacob reaped the consequences of the actions he had sown earlier. But he also received much blessing from God and learned of His care and mercy during a difficult time. Through difficult circumstances Jacob's faith in God grew. When at last he had to face Esau, the brother he had wronged, Jacob anticipated trouble and realized that he might be killed. Yet the night before their meeting, God came again to Jacob.

This time Jacob wrestled with God. In spite of an injured leg, Jacob hung on and said, "I will not let You go, unless You bless me" (Gen 32:26). He longed for God's blessing more than anything, for he finally trusted God to provide. So the Lord said to him, "Your name shall no longer be called Jacob, but Israel: for you have struggled with God and with men, and have prevailed" (32:28). When Jacob received the blessing he had requested, he gave God all the credit: "I have seen God face to face, and my life is preserved" (Gen 32:30).

Have you wrestled with God? You and I must have faith in order to be born again, but often our faith remains weak because we have never wrestled with God. Wrestling in this context does not indicate resistance to God. As His children we must wrestle with Him about the truths of His Word and proclaim like Jacob, "Lord, I will not let You go until You make me know these truths, until You teach me how to apply them and how to be more like Christ!"

God brought Jacob to the end of his rope once again when he was compelled in his old age to make a journey to Egypt. Just as Jacob had once tricked his own father, his own sons had deceived him into believing his favorite son Joseph was dead. Yet now, after many years of grief, his sons had changed their story. Joseph was alive, they said, and ruling Egypt! What? Such a thing was impossible! Yet Jacob learned to trust God even in this strangest of situations. When father and son were reunited, Jacob's first utterance was to credit the promise God had given to preserve his children.

> Then Jacob said to Joseph: "God Almighty appeared to me at Luz in the land of Canaan and blessed me, and said to me, 'Behold, I will make you fruitful and multiply you, and I will make of you a multitude of people, and give this land to your descendants after you as an everlasting possession.'" (Gen. 48:3-4)

Now at the end of his life, Jacob's trust in God was complete. As the writer to the Hebrews recalls and the Old Testament relates (Gen. 48: 5-20), the patriarch gave a blessing to the two sons of Joseph, Ephraim and Manasseh. They, too, were now included in the promise God had given first to Abraham and had confirmed in turn to Isaac and Jacob.

Why did the writer to the Hebrews view Jacob's blessing as so significant? Simply put, it was because Jacob acted by faith. Consider his situation. Although he had once lived in the Promised Land, Jacob had been a nomad there. Now his sons and their households were in Egypt, a long way from Canaan. Yet Jacob fully expected that God would someday give the Promised Land to his descendants. Fulfillment of God's promise would have seemed impossible; in fact, it would ultimately take centuries. But Jacob had faith. He trusted God. He was so certain God would fulfill His promise that he instructed his sons to make sure he would be buried in Canaan (Gen. 47:29-31, 49:29-32).

Jacob saw in advance something that others would see only in hindsight. And it was because of this faith that he could give his Lord true worship, even with death closing upon him. Thus did the writer to the Hebrews say of Jacob and his forefathers, "These all died in faith, not having received the promises, but having seen them afar off were assured of them" (Hebrews 11:13).

JACOB EXPRESSED HIS FAITH

The blessing Jacob gave his grandsons Ephraim and Manasseh is significant as a demonstration of faith. The content of that blessing is also important. For one thing, it defied all normal expectations.

> Then Israel stretched out his right hand and laid it on Ephraim's head, who was the younger, and his left hand on Manasseh's head, guiding his hands knowingly, for Manasseh was the firstborn.... Now when Joseph saw that his father laid his right hand on the head of Ephraim, it displeased him; so he took hold of his father's hand to remove it from Ephraim's head to Manasseh's head. And Joseph said to his father, "Not so, my father, for this one is the firstborn; put your right hand on his head." (Gen. 48:14-18)

When Joseph pointed out the irregularity in the blessing, "his father refused" (Gen. 48:19) to stop. What was going on here? Jacob was himself a younger son who maneuvered to take the birthright of his brother Esau. Look what had resulted because of his action! Had Jacob not learned his lesson?

Now, the two reversals were distinctly different, however. Rather than reversing the usual custom through trickery, Jacob did so through his trust in God. Earlier in the conversation he had expressed his acceptance of both grandsons by proclaiming, "[They] *are* mine" (48: 5). When he gave the right hand of blessing the younger child, Jacob answered Joseph's reproach by saying he was certain of God's plan.

> I know, my son, I know: [Manasseh] also shall become a people, and he also shall be great: but truly his younger brother [Ephraim] shall be greater than he, and his descendants shall become a multitude of nations. (Gen. 48:19).

Jacob knew this blessing was God's will, and he stood squarely upon that knowledge—even though, given his past, he may have thus laid himself open for criticism. Nevertheless, Jacob "blessed them that day...and he set Ephraim before Manasseh" (48:14-20).

Centuries later, this prophecy of God through Jacob was proven true. The descendants of Ephraim became the leaders of Israel's ten northern tribes, while the tribe of Manasseh divided.

The writer to the Hebrews records, finally, that Jacob blessed Joseph's grandsons "and worshiped." (Jacob's act of worship actually preceded the blessing. Nevertheless, the two events occurred close together during the patriarch's final days.)

> When the time drew near that Israel must die, he called his son Joseph and said to him, "Now if I have found favor in your sight, please put your hand under my thigh". So Israel bowed himself on the head of the bed. (Gen. 47:29,31)

His physical strength had waned. He needed help to sit up. He was so weak, apparently, that he had to lean on his staff (Heb. 11: 21) even to sit on the edge of his bed. He could no longer imagine it possible to do any mighty deeds to impress God and gain His favor. In fact, his life was nearly over. Yet as Jacob leaned on his staff, he did the best thing any man could ever do. In his heart, as in his body, he was prostrate before God. This is the attitude of true worship, that of a heart that is humbled in complete submission before God.

The New Testament's Hall of Faith records this scene because, even for us today, it is a powerful lesson and a great encouragement. At one time this man had acted and schemed as if all success depended on him. But in the end, Jacob humbled himself before God. He had learned to trust God instead of himself. Lovingly, the Lord had allowed Jacob to experience many trials and blessings in order to bring His child into a vibrant relationship with Him. God does the same for us today! If you and I trust Him fully, as Jacob did, we will naturally worship the Object of our trust until the end of our days.

THINGS TO THINK ABOUT

1. List the ways that God worked through Jacob's life to teach him complete faith and trust in the Lord.

2. How did Jacob, who had always relied on himself, at last demonstrate that he trusted that God could provide what he needed?

3. What lesson can you learn from Jacob's wrestling match with God? How does this encounter apply to your life today?

4. Why did the writer to the Hebrews choose Jacob's dying actions as the single example of his faith? Explain in your own words.

5. How did Jacob, through his giving of a blessing and through the content of that blessing, demonstrate his faith?

23

TRUE WORSHIP BOWS BEFORE THE CREATOR

THE LIVING CREATURES • REV. 4:1-11

The twenty-four elders fall down before Him who sits on the throne and worship Him who lives forever and ever, and cast their crowns before the throne, saying: "You are worthy, O Lord, to receive glory and honor and power; for You created all things, and by Your will they exist and were created."

We began our study of worship in Genesis with the first recorded act of worship in the Bible. God accepted the worship of Abel, but not of his brother Cain; God could see the conditions of their hearts. In fact, the pattern has been the same throughout the rest of the Bible. God instructs and encourages mankind to fall before Him in worship. Some people do; most do not.

Now we come to the last book of the Bible. Our study has covered centuries of time. Through it all God has pleaded with men to turn to Himself, even as He pleads today. How long will He keep on pleading? The Book of Revelation makes clear, sadly, that when time is coming to its end, humanity still will not have learned its lesson. For the book records prophecy not only of true worship from right hearts, but also of false idolatrous worship. Tragically, those who ignored His pleading, who preferred false worship because they did not have true faith in God, will become the objects of His final and immeasurable wrath.

THE THRONE ROOM

The apostle John was among the most privileged persons ever to live. God invited this choice servant to see a glimpse of His glory. Christ had earlier commanded John to "write the things which you have seen, and the things which are, and the things which will take place after this" (Rev. 1:19). As the Revelation opens, John records the vision he is given of the glorified Christ (1:9-17) and of His letters to the seven churches (1:18-3:22). These letters constitute "the things which are." After recording these letters, at last John is invited to see and to begin recording "the things which will take place after this."

> After these things I looked, and behold, a door standing open in heaven. And the first voice which I heard was like a trumpet speaking with me, saying, "Come up here, and I will show you things which must take place after this." Immediately I was in the Spirit; and behold, a throne set in heaven, and One sat on the throne. (Rev. 4:1-2)

Notice that John himself did not open the door; God opened the door for him. No man can possibly force himself into the throne room of God! In the throne room the Lord spoke to John in a voice that the apostle could only liken to a trumpet, for he could not think of any other earthly sound that would compare to the authoritative voice of God. Perhaps most significantly of all, we learn in this passage that John will see things that *must* happen. And the unfolding record of the last days is one of terrible tribulation and judgment. These are not "might be" events! God today is holding back His full wrath, but one day it *must* be poured out against all sin and rebellion.

When John writes that he "was in the spirit," he is indicating that he was transported to heaven by the Holy Spirit. This is the only way in which anyone can ever get into heaven: to be taken there by God. The principle applies whether a person enters heaven to see a vision, as was the case with John, or whether he comes for eternal residence. Untold billions throughout the ages have hoped in their own human wisdom for a path to heaven, but God's way through salvation in Christ is still the only way.

Once in the throne room of God, John's natural and immediate response was obedience—that is, obedience to the command that he begin to write down what he saw. There were incomparable sights all around him! But the apostle's attention was riveted first to the throne and the One who sat upon it. The word "throne" is in fact one of the key words in the Book of Revelation. John mentions it in nearly every chapter. Its importance to the Revelation is evidenced by the fact that, of the sixty-two references to the word "throne" in the New Testament, forty-seven are in this final book. People who lived in Roman times had a true sense of the concept behind the word "throne." For them, the idea of a throne conveyed ultimate power and authority. When the Roman emperor handed down judgment from his throne, none could resist it.

Yet the majesty of God far surpassed even such a grand picture. John found that he could not adequately describe in human terms the One seated on the throne. The apostle tried to express what he saw with words human beings might understand:

> And He who sat there was like a jasper and a sardius stone in appearance; and there was a rainbow around the throne, in appearance like an emerald. (Rev. 4:3)

The One was "like" a jasper and sardius stone to look upon, and a rainbow that seemed "like" an emerald surrounded Him. Since terms used for precious stones have changed over the centuries, it is difficult to say exactly what John saw. As far as scholars can determine, jasper was probably a clear gem and sardine was red. But John's meaning is clear; the chief characteristic of the One sitting on the throne was brilliance like light. Moreover, an emerald-colored rainbow, seemingly a reminder of God's faithfulness, surrounded the throne. For after the flood that God used to destroy the world, He set His rainbow in the cloud, "the sign of a covenant between Me and the earth...[that] the waters shall never again become a flood to destroy all flesh" (Gen. 9:13-15).

In this context, the Book of Revelation, the rainbow carries added significance. God gave the bow in connection with a global catastrophe. The bow proclaims, "You can trust God." While that declaration means that God can be trusted not to destroy the earth again by a flood, it also means that He can be trusted to carry out His promises regarding the final worldwide conflagration described in the Revelation. He will judge the inhabitants of earth because of sin and then destroy this old, wicked world by fire (2 Pet. 3:10). He promised, to do so, and the rainbow is a reminder that God keeps His promises.

How long must John have marveled at the sight of the One upon the throne! How could any one of us have pulled our eyes away from that glory? But the apostle had been commanded to make a record of his vision, and so eventually he drew his gaze to another wondrous sight.

> Around the throne were twenty-four thrones, and on the thrones I saw twenty-four elders sitting, clothed in white robes; and they had crowns of gold on their heads. (Rev. 4:4)

Who are these elders? In the introductory passage of the Revelation, John notes that Christ "has made us kings and priests to His God and Father" (Rev. 1:6). Also, the Scriptures describe God's people as "a royal priesthood" (1 Pet. 2:9). Likely, the elders around the throne are representatives of the priesthood of believers from both the Old and New Testament eras. A precedent for this conclusion is King David's dividing of the Levitical priesthood into twenty-four sections and appointing an elder for each (1 Chron. 24:7-19).

John's description of the elders provides three more clues that suggest they are representatives of the redeemed. First, they will have seats of their own. In fact, the Word of God promises to all the redeemed that "we shall also reign with him" (2 Tim. 2:12). Second, the elders will be clothed in white. Later in Revelation we find that white robes will be the raiment given to those who obtain redemption in Christ during the Great Tribulation (7:13-14). Third, the elders will wear crowns such as God has promised to reward to the faithful (1 Tim. 4:8; 1 Cor. 9:25; 1 Thess. 2:19; James 1:12; 1 Pet. 5:4).

Next, John records that "from the throne proceeded lightnings, thunderings, and voices" (Rev. 4:5). Such imagery is frequently used in the Bible to describe the voice and power of God, often as a portent of His coming judgment. Job observed, "How small a whisper we hear of Him! But the thunder of His power who can understand?" He asked his friends,

"Have you an arm like God? Or can you thunder with a voice like His?" (Job 26:14, 40:9). Likewise, the prophet Samuel declared, "The adversaries of the LORD shall be broken in pieces; from heaven He will thunder against them. The LORD will judge the ends of the earth" (1 Sam. 2:10).

Before the throne John saw "seven lamps of fire burning before the throne, which are the seven Spirits of God" (Rev. 4:5). What did he mean? What are the *seven* Spirits of God? In the Bible, the number seven pictures completion or perfection. Therefore the seven Spirits of God are the complete revelation of the Holy Spirit. Until now, John has described the One upon the throne as having attributes of both God the Father and God the Son. Now we see that, as final judgment is being prepared, God the Holy Spirit is also represented.

The awesome description continues as John observes that "before the throne there was a sea of glass, like crystal" (4:6). Although the nature of this sea is open to different interpretations, it almost certainly is a symbol of God's perfect purity and holiness. Perhaps the sea of glass also provides a kind of buffer zone around the throne, a reminder to everyone present that God is holy and completely removed from any kind of sin.

HEAVENLY BEINGS WORSHIP HIM

Earthly beings—the redeemed of all the ages—are represented before the throne through their elders. But John notes that "in the midst of the throne, and around the throne," heavenly beings will be present as well.

The King James Bible calls these beings four "beasts." Although a better translation would be "living creatures," John does make them sound pretty strange! They are "full of eyes around and within," perhaps symbolizing their knowledge, wisdom, or ability to observe. Each of the four creatures has its own unique qualities, however. One is like a lion, considered in the ancient world to be the mightiest of wild creatures. The second is like a calf or a bull, considered the mightiest of domesticated beasts. The third is like an eagle, the mightiest of all birds. And the fourth resembles a man, the image of God. Whatever these creatures are, God created them for His service. Thus it is not surprising to learn that they share some traits of the cherubim and seraphim that Ezekiel and Isaiah saw (Ezek. 10:1-22, Is. 6:1-7). In fact, even as Isaiah recorded, the words of these heavenly beings are paeans to the holiness of the One upon the throne.

> And they do not rest day or night, saying: "Holy, holy, holy, Lord God Almighty, Who was and is and is to come!" Whenever the living creatures give glory and honor and thanks to Him who sits on the throne, who lives forever and ever. (Rev. 4:8b-9)

Note the content of their worship. Even these heavenly beings will exalt God for His holiness, power, and eternality. By giving God *glory*, they will acknowledge His magnificence and confess His might. By giving God honor that is rooted in proper respect and fear, these heavenly beings will confess His value. And by giving God thanks, they will bow to Him as their Creator. Their thankfulness will be recognition of God's grace, mercy, and kindness—and of their own dependence on those traits. After all, it is He who sits on the throne and lives forever. Who can resist One who reigns forever? Who can outlive or outlast Him? These heavenly beings set a good example of true worship.

God's People Worship Him

Once the four heavenly beings have worshiped God, next the twenty-four elders will worship Him. They do not shout or dance. They do not resort to ritual or tradition. As representatives of all who owe their salvation to God alone, how do these elders express themselves in worship?

> [They] fall down before Him who sits on the throne and worship Him who lives forever and ever, and cast their crowns before the throne. (Rev. 4:10)

Consider that the twenty-four elders are themselves rulers who sit upon thrones of their own. They represent countless millions of people. But their status makes no difference to them. They, too, are redeemed! As one they will fall before God and cast their crowns at His feet. The crowns were given to them as rewards, but without hesitation, keeping nothing for themselves, they will give all the credit to God. The twenty-four elders are so thankful for His mercy and love that the natural expression of their hearts is to humble themselves before God. Their example of true worship is a good model for us to follow.

True worship is first proved by the elders' actions: they fall before God and cast their crowns before His throne. Because their hearts are right, their words will also demonstrate true worship.

> You are worthy, O Lord, to receive glory and honor and power; for You created all things, And by Your will they exist and were created. (Rev. 4:11)

God alone is worthy to receive all acclaim from every living creature, heavenly or earthly. Why is He alone worthy? The elders give two reasons: God *creates* all things and, at His pleasure, He *sustains* all things. Should not the things created and sustained by God show genuine thankfulness to Him? Or should we not honor His holiness? Should we live life only for our own pleasure?

John's picture of God's great throne room is a kind of snapshot of the moments just before the final outpouring of His wrath. When all is said and done, God's Word affirms, "at the name of Jesus every knee should bow, of those in heaven, and of those on earth, and of those under the earth" (Phil. 2:10). Every created being will someday worship the One upon the throne. Some will do so as they beg for mercy, having rejected God's free gift of salvation until it became too late. Others will worship God freely, thankful for their redemption and continuing the true worship they gave Him in this life.

Which kind of worshiper would you rather be?

THINGS TO THINK ABOUT

1. Why is it significant that the door to heaven was opened *for* John and that his transportation to heaven was not his own?

2. Put into your own words the attributes of God that John described and the meaning of those attributes.

3. How do you know that all three Persons of the Triune God are on the throne? Why is this fact important in light of the beginning of the final judgment?

4. Describe in your own words how the worship of the heavenly beings can be an example for our worship.

5. Why will the twenty-four elders cast their crowns at the feet of God?

24

True Worship
Bows Before the
Lamb

The Heavenly Host • Rev. 7:9-17

*[A] great multitude which no one could number...[was]
standing before the throne and before the Lamb...and crying
out with a loud voice, saying, "Salvation belongs to our God
who sits on the throne, and to the Lamb!"*

I have been privileged to visit some of the oldest and most beautiful
churches in the world. I have seen the soaring architecture, the
paintings and frescoes, the mahogany choir lofts, the pulpits
inlaid with gold, and the marble altars. In my mind's eye I can almost
see the pomp and pageantry of these churches as they would have
been of old—the nervous young acolytes, the chanting choir, the
solemn bishops in their grand array. And above all these, the great
organ would fill the cavernous space with a music that is both felt and
heard. Who would not be carried aloft in such a setting, we might ask,
to a realm beyond the mundane cares of this world?

Yet even these scenes do not compare with the awesome grandeur
witnessed by the apostle John as he continued to record "the things
which shall be" in heaven at the end of the ages. This revelation begins
in the very throne room of God, where wondrous heavenly beings and
the honored elders of the redeemed will give Him worship (Rev. 4). At

last "the great day of His wrath is come" (6:17). Six terrible judgments will be loosed upon the world, and then will follow a pause before the seventh and final judgment. During that pause, John beheld "a great multitude, which no man could number" (7:9), standing before the throne and worshiping God with grateful hearts.

What a magnificent scene! But who are these people that will be privileged to come into the throne room of God? Why will they honor Him and how will their honor of Him find expression in their worship? God has recorded their example in His Word for our instruction. What can we learn?

A PICTURE OF WORSHIP

No man will be able to number the multitude John beheld, but it is awe-inspiring and yet comforting to realize that God can number that multitude, for "the Lord knows those who are His" (2 Tim. 2:19). The immeasurable size of the multitude is doubly comforting when we realize that it confirms that, to the end of all time, God will keep His promise to Abraham: "I will multiply your descendants as the stars of the heaven, and as the sand which is on the seashore" (Gen. 22:17).

Is the multitude, then, the Jewish nation? No, for the multitude comes from "all nations, tribes, people, and tongues" (Rev. 7:9). So the multitude will include Gentiles as well as Jews. But heaven is the abode only of those who have been redeemed through Christ. Then who makes up this great crowd? Remember that God's covenant with Abraham included the promise that "in you all the nations of the earth shall be blessed" (Gen. 22:18). Out of Abraham's line would come a Messiah to save God's people. But who are His people?

> Therefore know that only those who are of faith are sons of Abraham...[for] to Abraham and his Seed were the promises made. He does not say, "And to seeds," as of many; but as of one, "And to your seed," who is Christ....And if you are Christ's, then you are Abraham's seed, and heirs according to the promise. (Gal. 3:7-9)

Yet another clue to the identity of the multitude is found in John's description of the people's appearance. They look like victors, for they are "clothed with white robes" (Rev. 7:9). In the ancient world white robes were often given to the victors in athletic games and military battles. Furthermore, the people will be holding "palms in their hands," a common custom at joyous celebrations. God Himself instructed the Israelites to celebrate their deliverance from Egyptian bondage by taking "branches of palm trees....[A]nd you shall rejoice, He commanded them" (Lev. 23:40). Palm branches likewise figured significantly in Jesus' triumphal entry into Jerusalem (John 12:13).

To summarize, the multitude will include both Jews and Gentiles, children of Abraham's promise through faith in Christ, men and women who are in victorious, joyful celebration. Little wonder that John records that the multitude was "crying out with a loud voice, saying, 'salvation belongs to our God who sits on the throne, and to the Lamb!'" (Rev. 7:10).

Who is the Lamb? His coming was prophesied by Isaiah, who proclaimed, "The LORD has laid on Him the iniquity of us all. He was oppressed, and He was afflicted, yet He opened not His mouth: He was led as a lamb to the slaughter" (Is. 53:6-7). His arrival was announced by John the Baptist, who declared, "Behold the Lamb of God, who takes away the sin of the world" (John 1:29). And John the apostle records in the Revelation that "in the midst of the throne...stood a Lamb as though it had been slain" (Rev. 5:6), at whose appearing the living creatures and elders will sing,

> You were slain, and have redeemed us to God by Your blood out of every tribe and tongue and people and nation, and have made us kings and priests to our God; and we shall reign on the earth. (Rev. 5:9-10)

Then "with a loud voice" an innumerable host of angels will join in the song:

> "Worthy is the Lamb who was slain to receive power and riches and wisdom and strength and honor and glory and blessing!" (Rev. 5:12)

This Lamb is Jesus, for what John records next was prophesied in the Scriptures: "At the name of Jesus every knee should bow, of those in heaven, and of those on earth, and of those under the earth; and that every tongue should confess that Jesus Christ is Lord" (Phil. 2:10-11). Now to the apostle John is given the privilege of seeing this word fulfilled.

> And every creature which is in heaven and on the earth and under the earth and such as are in the sea, and all that are in them, I heard saying: "Blessing and honor and glory and power Be to Him who sits on the throne, and to the Lamb, forever and ever!" (Rev. 5:13)

Sadly for untold millions, this recognition will come too late. They denied Christ in life but, once the Lamb is revealed upon His throne for all to see, they will be able to deny Him no longer. At this point in John's record, God's judgment is only moments away—and then it is unleashed! After six successive judgments the wicked of the earth will at last "[say] to the mountains, 'Fall on us and hide us from the face of Him who sits on the throne and from the wrath of the Lamb'" (Rev. 6:16).

And this cry of the wicked brings us back to the pause before the seventh and final judgment, and to the uncounted multitude who will be arrayed in celebration around the throne. How infinitely better it is that they will honor the Lamb in joyous victory than that, like the wicked, acknowledge His Lordship only under compulsion.

But again, who makes up this joyous multitude?

A PICTURE OF THE WORSHIPERS

We have established that the multitude will include Jews and Gentiles, and that it consists of children of Abraham's promise through faith in Christ. Then does this multitude comprise the redeemed of all the ages? No, for when this multitude arrives on the scene, the Church will already have been raptured to heaven (1 Thess. 4:13-18, Matt. 24:36-44) and will already be worshiping the Lamb through its representatives, the twenty-four elders. The identity of the multitude is revealed to John in a conversation.

> Then one of the elders answered, saying to me, "Who are these arrayed in white robes, and where did they come from?" And I said to him, "Sir, you know." So he said to me, "These are the ones who come out of the great tribulation, and washed their robes and made them white in the blood of the Lamb." (Rev. 7:13-14)

The time of the Great Tribulation will be horrific, but God has given you and me a special promise. That we might find comfort rather than distress as the end nears, we have His reassurance that "God did not appoint us to wrath" (1 Thess. 5:9). Indeed, when Christ introduced His Revelation to John, He gave the apostle a similar word of assurance. Jesus knew that John was about to behold unspeakably terrifying judgments. So He comforted John by telling him in advance, "Because you have kept My command to persevere, I also will keep you from the hour of trial which shall come upon the whole world, to test those who dwell on the earth" (Rev. 3:10).

For the present, Jesus has promised His Church, "In the world, you will have tribulation: but be of good cheer; I have overcome the world" (John 16:33). The Bible also gives us assurance that "as the sufferings of Christ abound in us, so our consolation also abounds through Christ" (2 Cor. 1:5). As Christians, you and I will suffer persecution, but we are assured that we have the Comforter to strengthen us. We also know that, if we are alive at the time of the Tribulation, we will be caught away to heaven before the Great Tribulation begins. The "Tribulation saints," however, will have none of these assurances.

It is significant, therefore, that when the Tribulation saints give credit to the Lamb for their salvation, all of heaven will join in their worship. The living creatures and elders and angels will have seen how these believers were martyred under the reign of Antichrist, being "slain for the word of God, and for the testimony which they held" (Rev. 6:9). Their testimony is all the more remarkable in light of the fact that God's Spirit will not be in the earth during the Tribulation. Through special witnesses given by God (see Rev. 7:1-8), these saints will come to a knowledge of the truth and despite great satanic delusion in the world. And then they will keep to their faith without the benefit of the indwelling of the Holy Spirit. So all of heaven will join their victory celebration, saying,

Amen! Blessing and glory and wisdom, thanksgiving and honor
and power and might, be to our God forever and ever. Amen.
(Rev. 7:12)

Even the angels will fall down and worship. They will never
experience the joy of salvation, but they love God and cannot help
joining the redeemed as they all worship their mutual Creator. The
elders, also, will fall down and worship, for they know personally
God's grace in salvation. You and I, also, when we read of the
Tribulation saints and their miraculous deliverance, should be
wondrously encouraged at the saving grace and power of the Lamb.
For these saints will be won the same way we are, through being
washed by the blood of Christ.

Although the Tribulation is not upon us, the signs of the times
suggest that events on earth may be rushing to their conclusion. The
Bible tells us that apostasy (2 Thess. 2:3), false teaching, and immorality
(Matt. 24:11-12) will increase as the end approaches. Even today, it is a
great miracle that people are still being saved. When we hear such news,
do we feel the same great joy, as do the hosts of heaven? Do we rejoice
in our hearts that God has granted salvation to another person? Do we
still marvel at the wonder of our own deliverance? And does our wonder
cause us to worship the Lamb, to attribute all things great and glorious
to Him, and to affirm these realities forever?

John's vision of the Tribulation saints concludes by recording what
will happen to this redeemed multitude. They will "serve [God] day and
night in His temple" (Rev. 7:15), and He will take care of all their needs.

They shall neither hunger anymore nor thirst anymore; the sun
shall not strike them, nor any heat; for the Lamb who is in the
midst of the throne will shepherd them and lead them to living
fountains of waters. And God will wipe away every tear from
their eyes. (Rev. 7:16-17)

The circumstances of these saints will certainly have changed
dramatically from the circumstances they experienced on earth! During
the Tribulation they will not be allowed to buy or sell, and so they will
experience hunger and thirst. They will be driven into the wilderness

and have no abode. But once they come into the presence of the Lamb, all of those circumstances will change. Their Savior will care for them.

Has not Jesus given you and me similar promises? "Come to Me, all you who labor and are heavy laden, and I will give you rest" (Matt. 11:28). "Blessed are those who hunger and thirst for righteousness: for they shall be filled" (Matt. 5:6). "In my Father's house are many mansions: if it were not so, I would have told you. I go to prepare a place for you" (John 14:2). "And God will wipe away every tear from their eyes; there shall be no more death, nor sorrow, nor crying. There shall be no more pain, for the former things have passed away" (Rev. 21:4).

A story is told of Amy Carmichael, the great missionary who endured long years of frail health until her death in 1951. A woman who visited Amy related to her own poor health, explaining how the doctor had warned, "Don't even bend over suddenly, or you might die on the spot." Amy gave a tart and twinkling reply: "However do you resist the temptation?" The mere thought of heaven, and of what the Lamb has done for us, should arouse in us great anticipation. And these thoughts should constrain us to fall before Him in true worship.

THINGS TO THINK ABOUT

1. How have you become a child of Abraham and an heir to the promise that God gave him?

2. How do you know that the Lamb upon the throne is Jesus Christ? What confirmation of His identity does the Bible give?

3. How do you know that the multitude before the throne comprises the "Tribulation saints"? What clues do the Scriptures provide?

4. Why can you be sure that, as a redeemed believer, you will be raptured to heaven and not go through the Great Tribulation?

5. How should the knowledge of Christ's return affect the way you live today? See 1 John 2:28-3:3 and 2 Peter 3:10-14.

TRUE WORSHIP REJOICES AT GOD'S TRIUMPH

THE ELDERS • REVELATION 11:15-18

*The kingdoms of this world have become the kingdoms of our
Lord and of His Christ, and He shall reign forever and ever!
And the twenty-four elders who sat before God on their thrones
fell on their faces and worshiped God.*

When *USA Today* first hit the newsstands, critics called it
the "McPaper," the journalistic equivalent of fast food.
Today, of course, its colorful graphics and brief articles
set the standard. Why is USA Today the new standard in American
journalism? The past two generations of Americans have been raised
on television and conditioned to process information that is highly
visual and easy to scan. Today's newspapers and magazines have
long since adapted to this new reality. In fact, now that the Internet
has introduced the concept of "interactive" mass communication,
some futurists wonder whether one-way media such as television
and newspapers can ultimately survive.

Television and mass media have also made their impact in the
pews on Sundays. Woe to the preacher whose sermon lasts more than
half an hour—or to the preacher who keeps his congregation late! More
than a century ago, D.L. Moody and Billy Sunday could hold a crowd

for hours with their oratory. But today even the most devout American Christian would have trouble sitting still for much more than an hour.

When our church put up a new building a few years ago, I had a computer port hooked up to the pulpit and a PowerPoint projector installed overhead. Now when I preach an expository sermon, our people can follow the outline on the screen behind me as an aid to their comprehension. Sometimes, to enhance their understanding I include a picture or a map that relates to the passage being taught. This approach might not be the old-fashioned way. But Americans are accustomed to processing information visually—and today's software makes it easy even for preachers to prepare effective presentations.

However, I know that somewhere I must draw the line. It would not be much more difficult to include a video clip or sound bite in my sermons. Nor would it be difficult to take questions from the congregation, or ask for testimonies as a way to encourage "dialogue" with the audience. But when do we cross over from sermon to spectacle, from exposition to entertainment? How much of our approach is an appropriate recognition of the way people derive meaning from a message today—and how much is an encouragement for people to become lazy in their attention to the scriptures?

If staying within proper boundaries for worship requires fallible human judgment, then it stands to reason that errors can and do occur—in either direction. On the one hand, churches can cling to liturgies and rituals from which the people gain little understanding of the One they have come to worship. On the other hand, the quest for relevance can lead preachers and congregations to associate worship with a certain amount of entertainment and emotion. If a man of God were to stand in the pulpit and simply to unfold the matchless wonders of the Almighty God, many people would be confused or bored. The inescapable conclusion is that, in the end, many are more impressed by human inventions than they are by God Himself.

If you and I are truly redeemed, however, then we must be humbled by what God has done for us. If we truly comprehended His grace and mercy toward us, short attention spans would not present a problem! The Revelation gives us a particularly sharp picture of God at work on our behalf. For the book is in effect the last chapter of

God's Book, the chapter in which we get to find out how the story ends. Now, as our study turns to the seventh and final outpouring of God's wrath upon the world, we see clearly that the Lord is taking the last steps to complete His plan for the ages. Those in heaven at this time will witness His full judgment against sin and Satan, then observe how God will reward His faithful servants. These scenes will impel the redeemed to bow in humble worship. I am looking forward to being there! But since God has already revealed to us knowledge of these things, should we not worship Him even today for His great works?

THE ANNOUNCEMENT

The first six judgments on the earth will take place as the Lamb opens the first six seals of a book, or scroll. But when He opens the seventh seal, something different will occur. Seven angels will come forward, all bearing trumpets whose successive blasts introduce judgments even more serious than the previous six "seal judgments." One by one, the "trumpet judgments" unfold. All of heaven—the saints and elders, the four living creatures and the great angel host— will witness an incomparably awesome display of God's power and wrath. Then, at last, everyone knows that the time has come for the seventh trumpet to herald God's final assault against sin and sinners. But the trumpet blast will be accompanied by an announcement.

> Then the seventh angel sounded: and there were loud voices in heaven, saying, "The kingdoms of this world have become the kingdoms of our Lord and of His Christ, and He shall reign forever and ever!" (Revelation 11:15)

This verse, of course, is the inspiration for the majestic "Hallelujah Chorus" of Handel's *Messiah*. But among the hosts of heaven this announcement will elicit a response that is even greater than that majestic chorus. This announcement, that the kingdoms of the world will be restored to Christ, is *the* announcement for which all of creation has been waiting! Since Adam and Eve first trusted Satan more than they trusted God, until the moment of this announcement, the kingdoms of this world have been under the rule of the enemy. Jesus Himself called

Satan "the ruler of this world" (John 14:30) and John affirmed that "the whole world *lies under the sway of* the wicked one" (1 John 5:19). Satan made no empty boast when he tempted Christ by "show[ing] Him all the kingdoms of the world and their glory. And he said to Him, 'All these things I will give You if You will fall down and worship me'" (Matt. 4: 8-9). The kingdoms of the world were Satan's to give.

How thankful we should be that Jesus did not yield to Satan's offer but chose to wait on His Father's timing! Jesus went on to endure even worse trial, the trial of the cross, so that all creation could be redeemed through His sacrifice. Now the Revelation displays the truth that God's final act of redemption will include giving the kingdoms of the world back to the rightful King. Of course, Christ reigns even now over the spiritual kingdom. But in the final redemption He will be restored as King of Kings. Scripture declares that the literal kingdoms of this world rightfully belong to this King of Kings. "The earth is the LORD's, and all its fullness; the world, and they those who dwell therein" (Ps. 24:1). God Himself proclaimed,

> I have set My King on My holy hill of Zion. I will declare the decree: The LORD has said to Me, "You are My Son, Today I have begotten You. Ask of Me, and I will give You the nations for Your inheritance, and the ends of the earth for Your possession." (Ps. 2:6-8)

The prophets of old, also, proclaimed this truth. Daniel wrote, "And in the days of these kings the God of heaven will set up a kingdom, which shall never be destroyed: and the kingdom shall not be left to other people; it shall break in pieces and consume all these kingdoms, and it shall stand forever" (Dan. 2:44). Similarly, it was revealed to Zechariah that "the LORD shall be King over all the earth. In that day it shall be—The LORD is one and His name one" (Zech. 14:9).

Interestingly, though Revelation describes future events, the announcement that the kingdoms of the world will be restored to Christ is made in the *past* tense. Even the grammar underlines the absolute certainty that full redemption will occur according to God's plan!

Some people today wonder where this mighty God is; they do not seem to see much evidence of Him. They ask why He has not come as He promised, and they equate God's patience with powerlessness. Peter addressed this issue in his second epistle, explaining that "scoffers will come in the last days, walking according to their own lusts, and saying, 'Where is the promise of His coming? For since the fathers fell asleep, all things continue as *they were* from the beginning of creation'" (2 Peter 3:3-4).

Yet the God who spoke the world into existence "by the same word [keeps it] in store, are reserved for fire until the day of judgment and perdition of ungodly men" (2 Peter 3:7). God is mighty in power regardless of anyone's opinion. The news that He will reveal His mighty power is good news to those who trust Him—but it is also an admonition. "[L]ooking forward to these things, be diligent to be found by Him in peace, without spot and blameless" (2 Peter 3:14).

The Response

Today it is fashionable even for theologians and scholars to dismiss the idea of a literal final judgment. Certainly, many insist a loving God could not condemn anyone to eternal agony. Such rigid justice would be no justice at all; it would be inherently unfair. People of all religions are sincerely striving in their own way to reach God, and He must surely recognize that fact. No person can claim a monopoly on the truth, and no Christian could rejoice in heaven knowing that others are in everlasting torment.

The Revelation, however, provides a picture of how those in heaven *will* react to God's final judgment upon the earth and the restoration of its kingdoms to the rightful Ruler. Of those who represent the redeemed before the throne of God it is written,

> And the twenty-four elders who sat before God on their thrones fell on their faces and worshiped God, saying: "We give You thanks, O Lord God Almighty, the One who is and who was and who is to come, because You have taken Your great power and reigned." (Rev. 11:16-17)

Do the elders really know what is coming? Are they really thankful for the millions who will die and be eternally condemned because of the massive judgment that God is about to bring to pass? Yes, for the Revelation confirms that the elders are aware that "the nations were angry, and Your wrath has come…and [God] should destroy those who destroy the earth" (Rev. 11:18). Then why do the elders give thanks? Because not only do they understand God, but they also understand His work.

Note, "the nations were angry." Even in Old Testament times David wondered, "Why do the nations rage and the people plot a vain thing? The kings of the earth set themselves, and the rulers take counsel together, against the LORD, and against His anointed" (Ps. 2:1-2). The world has always been angry with God! Yet mankind's innate consciousness of God, and since the time of the apostles, the ministry of the Holy Spirit, have restrained somewhat the full boldness of the wicked. During the Great Tribulation, however, their anger will no longer be suppressed. The world will vent its ultimate rage against God because of His full judgment against its sin.

For example, when God raises up two witnesses to spread the gospel, the world will celebrate their death "and not allow heir dead bodies to be put in graves. And those who dwell on the earth will rejoice over them, make merry, and send gifts to one another" (Rev. 11:9-10). Their intense hatred of these two gospel witnesses is in reality, of course, hatred toward God and His judgment of their sin. This hatred will develop into an all-out war against God. He will accommodate the world's hatred by gathering all of the nations for battle (Zech. 14:2). Literal combat will ensue, but the outcome of that combat is never in doubt; our Lord will be victorious (Rev. 19:11-21).

In the Great Tribulation, the world that rejected God and His Christ will at last show its true colors. At its final destruction, the elders will give thanks and worship their triumphant Lord. No one will question, at this point, how a Christian can be joyful in heaven when others are suffering in hell. Indeed, as the elders fall down before God and worship Him, they will do so in the knowledge that

> the time of the dead [is come], that they should be judged, and that You should reward Your servants the prophets and the saints, and those who fear Your name, small and great. (Rev. 11:18)

All men will have their due from God, whether for good or ill. In fact, this truth is explicitly affirmed at least thirty-four times in the Bible. Repeatedly, God promises that He will recompense all people for their deeds. Those who spurned His Lamb and chose to perish in their sins will be raised for their final sentencing, for "the dead were judged according to their works, by the things which were written in the books" (Rev. 20:12). Judgment will come also to those who in life threw themselves on the mercy of God and the atoning sacrifice of the Lamb. But their judgment will be for reward rather than for condemnation (2 Cor. 5:10, 1 Cor. 3:13-15).

The twenty-four elders will worship God as they rejoice in His triumph. Do you and I rejoice in His coming triumph as well? Does the thought that God will judge sin and restore rightful rule cause us to give thanks and bow before His great power? God's Word gives us marvelous details about His work in the last days. If our worship is true, it will illustrate knowledge of what God *has* done and of what He *will* do to complete His plan of redemption.

THINGS TO THINK ABOUT

1. Why must the kingdoms of the world be *restored* to Christ? How do you know that Satan is their present ruler?

2. If Satan is the present ruler of the world's kingdoms, how does that reality affect the way you must live as a Christian today?

3. How does the certainty that the world's kingdoms will be restored to Christ affect the way you live as a Christian today?

4. How would you answer people who scoff at the idea of final judgment, pointing out that the world continues today as it had always done?

5. How would you answer people who dismiss the idea of final judgment because they say it is horrifying and unfair?

TRUE WORSHIP PRAISES GOD'S JUDGMENTS

*Who shall not fear You, O Lord, and glorify Your name? For You
alone are holy. For all nations shall come and worship before
You, for Your judgments have been manifested.*

Jonathan Edwards, the great eighteenth-century preacher, is
widely considered the greatest theologian that America has ever
produced. What is more important, his study of the Word drove
him to a deep knowledge of God and to an intimate relationship with
Him. Sadly, many theologians since Edwards's time have become
proud in their own human scholarship and have fallen away from
God. In contrast to them, the more Jonathan Edwards knew of God's
Word, the closer he drew to its Author.

It is one of the great ironies of church history that, even though
Edwards was used of God to spark a great revival in America, his own
congregation put him out of their pulpit. Why? Because in obedience
to Scripture he sought to protect the communion table from those who
had reputations for practicing sin without repentance and confession.

People in every age become uneasy when their sins are pointed
out. They feel uncomfortable talking of God's judgment and
impending wrath. We do not like to think about such things. We like a

kind and benevolent God, One who does nice things to people who do not deserve His favor, simply because He is so good. We want a God who is in touch with His emotional side. Jonathan Edwards offered a very different picture of God in his preaching:

> The wrath of God is like great waters that are dammed for the present: they increase more and more, and rise higher and higher, till outlet is given; and the higher the stream is stopped, the more rapid and mighty is its course when once it is let loose. If God should only withdraw his hand from the floodgate, it would immediately fly open, and the fiery floods of the fierceness and wrath of God would rush forth with inconceivable fury, and would come upon you with omnipotent power; and if your strength were ten thousand times greater than it is, yea, ten thousand times greater than the strength of the stoutest, sturdiest devil in hell, it would be nothing to withstand or endure it.

The Bible confirms that the world must seek elsewhere for a god who overlooks sin and refuses to bring wrongdoing to justice. God is love. God is merciful. God is gracious. But God is also just. "For if God did not spare the angels who sinned…and did not spare the ancient world, but saved Noah,…then the Lord knows how to deliver the godly out of temptations, and to reserve the unjust under punishment for the day of judgment" (2 Pet. 2:4-9). God's wrath against sin is building, and it will continue to build until it is poured out against the stubborn rebels who refuse Him.

Something in our souls desires to separate the concept of worship from the picture of God pouring out His angry judgment on sin. Yet the Revelation displays redeemed saints falling before this God in worship as they praise Him for His wrath against sinners. True worship recognizes that God is offended by sin and praises Him for rendering justice against it.

THE SIGN IN HEAVEN

As the fifteenth chapter of Revelation opens, John writes that God allowed him to see "another sign in heaven, great and marvelous" (15:1).

God used signs often throughout history to gain the attention of human beings. For example, God gave the sign of the burning bush to Moses when He promised to deliver His people from Egyptian bondage. God also gave a sign to Gideon when He consumed his offering with fire, to validate His promise of deliverance from the Midianites.

This kind of signs is not prevalent in the New Testament. In fact, the word that refers to such signs appears only in the Revelation. Two signs are described in the twelfth chapter, and the final one is described in the fifteenth. However, since John describes this final sign as great and marvelous, we must conclude that it points to something very significant. What John sees is not a burning bush but rather "seven angels having the seven last plagues." The plagues are contained in bowls, and John records that "in them the wrath of God is complete" (15:1). The phrase "filled up" means "made complete" and indicates a final ending. This great and marvelous sign of the seven angels, therefore, introduces the final outpouring of God's wrath against the sinful world.

When John writes here about God's wrath, it is significant that he uses a Greek word that connotes an outward expression of inward anger. Usually the word "wrath" suggests a slow, inward, boiling indignation. But in this case, "the wrath of God" describes the outworking of that anger in words or actions. Sin truly makes God angry, and the Bible records this fact repeatedly. "God's anger was aroused" because of Balaam's stubbornness (Num. 22:22). Moses warned the Israelites to avoid idolatry, for to worship idols is "evil in the sight of the LORD your God, to provoke Him to anger" (Deut. 4:25). The Israelites were to flee idolatry, "lest the anger of the LORD your God be aroused against you, and destroy you from the face of the earth" (Deut. 6:15).

It is important to understand that God's anger is expressed against people. When David wondered whether people could sin and get away with it ("Shall they escape by iniquity?"), God inspired him to write the answer: "In anger cast down the peoples, O God" (Ps. 56:7). Jesus affirmed this truth when He taught that anyone who "does not believe the Son shall not see life, but the wrath of God abides on him" (John 3: 36). Another New Testament passage warns that "the wrath of God is revealed from heaven against all ungodliness and unrighteousness of men, who suppress the truth in unrighteousness" (Romans 1:18).

Sin makes God angry, and He expresses that anger in judgment against real people. But it is also true that God's anger against sin has been building. "But in accordance with your hardness and your impenitent heart you are treasuring up for yourself wrath in the day of wrath and revelation of the righteous judgment of God" (Rom. 2:5). How foolish and stubborn we can be, continuing in sin even though to do so builds up God's wrath against us!

If God bides His time, men think they have gotten away with their sin. But "what if God, wanting to show His wrath, and to make His power known, endured with much longsuffering the vessels of wrath prepared for destruction?" (Rom. 9:22). To the one who persists in his sin and in taunting God, the Word of God says, "Have you not asked those who travel the road?…[F]or the wicked are reserved for the day of doom; They shall be brought out on the day of wrath" (Job 21:29-30).

In American churches today, the general practice is to take a light view of sin. Such an outlook is then reflected in our worship. We believe that we must be affirmed in our sense of self-worth in order to live a vibrant Christian life. Often we hear the maxim, "You cannot love your neighbor as yourself if you do not love yourself!" The old fire-and-brimstone preaching is frowned on. It insults the intelligence of the hearers, makes them feel defeated, and drives them away from the church. They do not want to hear it!

But the Revelation records that God's wrath is coming. The seven plagues about to be loosed in final judgment include loathsome sores (Rev. 16:2), the turning of the seas and then the fresh water into blood (16:3-4), heat and fire, (16:8), darkness and pain (16:10), the drying up of the great Euphrates River so that the armies of the world may be gathered for Armageddon (16:12), and the worst earthquake and hail in history (16:18). John says that this judgment is the *telos*. This word is the word Jesus spoke on the cross when He said, "It is finished." The great sign of the seven angels, then, is the filling up of the full measure of God's anger. Men will try to hide from God in that day, but He will not cease until His wrath is completely spent on sinful people.

THE SONG IN HEAVEN

After John saw the seven angels holding bowls full of God's complete wrath, he reported,

> And I saw something like a sea of glass mingled with fire, and those who have the victory over the beast, over his image and over his mark and over the number of his name, standing on the sea of glass, having harps of God. (Rev. 15:2)

John described a similar sea in heaven surrounding the throne of God (Rev. 4:6). In both cases, we might conclude that the crystalline quality of these seas represents purity from sin. If so, this sea of glass will be a fitting place for the redeemed people of the Tribulation to stand before God. The sea is also "mingled with fire," a representation of the fact that they will have come through fiery trials. When the Antichrist and his minions put these "nonconformists" to death, they will claim final victory over narrow-minded, bigoted, intolerant religion. Yet the martyrdom of these saints will actually result in their victory! In the same way, Satan thought he had won the victory when Christ was crucified. But he was wrong. For Christ's death was His victory over our sins, through which victory we too are delivered.

Little wonder that these Tribulation saints, "having the harps of God," will start to sing "the song of Moses" and "the song of the Lamb" (15:2-3) We do not know what the song of the Lamb will be, although clearly it will be a song of praise to Christ for His sacrifice. The song of Moses, however, has a precedent in Scripture. This "servant of God" (15:2) sang a song at the end of his wilderness journey, just before God took him home. "Then Moses spoke in the hearing of all the assembly of Israel, the words of this song until they were ended" (Deut. 31:30).

In this song, Moses praises God as faithful and dependable (Deut. 32:1-6), and as a God who provides for His people (7-14) in spite of the fact that they are often unthankful (15-18) and would later prove unfaithful. God would punish His people by displaying His love for the Gentiles, thus moving Israel to jealousy (19-21), and by bringing calamity upon Israel (22-35). Moses' song ends by declaring that God will redeem His own (36-39) and take vengeance on His enemies (41).

Like the song of Moses, the song sung by those redeemed from the Tribulation will praise God for His might and power.

> They sing the song of Moses, the servant of God, and the song of the Lamb, saying: "Great and marvelous are Your works, Lord God Almighty! Just and true are Your ways, O King of the saints! Who shall not fear You, O Lord, and glorify Your name? For You alone are holy. For all nations shall come and worship before You, for Your judgments have been manifested." (Rev. 15:3-4)

This joyous song acknowledges God's great works, mighty power, justice, authority, and holiness. The phrase "King of the saints," however, requires some clarification. Greek manuscripts differ over whether the text says that God reigns over His saints, or the nations, or the ages. The best evidence is in favor of nations; the second best is for the ages. Yet it is true that God in His mighty power reigns over all three—nations, ages, and saints.

The saints singing in heaven teach the very important lesson that praise from redeemed people does not focus on self. There is no hint that anyone in heaven will complain about God's judgment on sin and sinners (although many on earth today are aghast at the thought of such judgment). None of the redeemed will complain that God allowed them to experience persecution in the Tribulation (although many today complain about their difficult circumstances and blame God for them).

To hear some people today who call themselves Christians, one would think their heavenly refrain would be "Nobody knows the trouble I've seen!" A far better idea of the saints' song in heaven is communicated by the old gospel hymn that is still sung in many churches:

> *I have a song I love to sing,*
> *Since I have been redeemed,*
> *Of my Redeemer, Savior, King,*
> *Since I have been redeemed.*
>
> *Since I have been redeemed,*
> *Since I have been redeemed,*
> *I will glory in His name;*

Since I have been redeemed,
I will glory in my Savior's name."

The song of the saints in heaven will conclude that God is worthy to be feared. That fear is founded on an awesome respect for God's person and power, as well as a dread of losing fellowship with the One who loves us. A right view of God compels us to glorify and reflect Him in what we think, say, and do. And this truth leads to a question: If you are uncomfortable or resentful with God for pouring out His just wrath in judgment against sin, how will you have a place in heaven with people who will praise His name because of that very same wrath? Indeed, how can you give God true worship today?

THINGS TO THINK ABOUT

1. Describe in your own words the concept of God's wrath. What does it mean? What is its object? How is it expressed?

2. God's wrath can build over time. Why is that truth important to share with a world that thinks it can get away with sin?

3. Preaching that makes people fearful of judgment is often frowned upon today. Why do you think people are wary of such preaching?

4. Read the "Song of Moses" in Deuteronomy 32. What are its parallels to the song of the saints in Revelation 15:3-4?

5. If the saints in heaven praise God for judging sin, should our worship praise Him for the same reason? How should we praise Him for His judgment of sin?

TRUE WORSHIP ANTICIPATES CHRIST'S RETURN

JOHN AND THE ANGEL • REV. 22:6-11

Behold, I am coming quickly! Blessed is he who keeps the words of the prophecy of this book. Now I, John, saw and heard these things. And when I heard and saw, I fell down to worship.

As a teenager I knew right from wrong. But there were times that I wanted to fit in and go with the crowd. So I would try to convince my parents that it was okay to go to a certain place with the kids from school. Everybody was doing it, so it must be all right. But dad or mom would look at me and say, "What if the Lord comes back while you are there?" I knew they were right, but I used to think that that question was their way of ruining my fun.

When I was a little older and pondered the Lord's return, sometimes I would think, "But let me get married first!" Even now I occasionally catch myself wishing my sons would give me grandchildren before the Rapture comes.

In both cases, my attitude about Christ's return was not biblical. For Jesus taught in several parables how important it is for servants to be ready for the Master's return. This instruction is made explicit in the admonitions to "abide in him; that when He appears, we may have

confidence and not be ashamed before Him at His coming" (1 John 2:
28). "Looking forward to these things," we are to "be diligent to be
found by Him in peace, without spot, and blameless" (2 Pet. 3:14).

Also, the Bible teaches that we should find comfort in the
prospect of our Lord's return (1 Thess. 4:16-18). Indeed, our love for
Jesus should be so great that His near return is our fondest hope. Paul
expressed this outlook when he wrote, "Finally, there is laid up for me
the crown of righteousness, which the Lord, the righteous Judge, will
give me on that Day: and not to me only, but to all who have loved His
appearing" (2 Tim. 4:8).

Jesus taught repeatedly that it is not for us to know when our
Master will return (Luke 12:40, 46; 21:34; Matt. 24:44; 25:13). In fact,
He said, "But of that day and hour no one knows, not even the angels
of heaven, but My Father only" (Matt. 24:36). The reality of Christ's
imminent return—and the idea that we must be ready for it at every
moment—should affect the way we think, talk, and live. It should also
affect the way we worship. Would we want Jesus to find us occupied
in mere "religion" when He returns? Or in worship that is more
concerned with meeting our own needs than with glorifying Him? Or
in worship in a place where His Word is denied? Of course not!

Some of the last words in God's Revelation to John emphasize
the imminent return of Christ and the need for His servants to faithfully
keep His words. As John himself learned in this passage, when we are
tempted to allow our worship to become skewed, the principles of the
Word of God correct us and drive us to true worship.

CHRIST WILL RETURN

In the opening of the Book of Revelation, Jesus Christ "sent and
signified [this Revelation] by His angel to His servant John" (1:1).
The apostle faithfully wrote all he saw and heard, then at last drew
his record to a close by reiterating that God "sent His angel to show
His servants the things which must shortly take place" (22:6). Next
John provided a brief epilogue that begins and ends with what are
essentially the same statements made by Jesus Himself: "Behold, I am
coming quickly" (22:7) and "Surely, I am coming quickly" (22:20).

Clearly, this point that bears great emphasis; it is almost as if Christ is saying, "Let me leave you with this thought!"

During His earthly ministry, Jesus, as noted above, encouraged His disciples to be ready for His return. Writing between 45 and 50 A.D., James taught fellow Christians that "the coming of the Lord is at hand" (5:8). In the year 51, Paul wrote to the Thessalonians that "we who are alive *and* remain shall be caught up together with them in the clouds to meet the Lord in the air" (1 Thess. 4:17). Paul used the pronoun "we" in this passage because he expected to be alive when Christ returned. He was still anticipating that great day when five years later he advised the Corinthians that "the time *is* short" (1 Cor. 7:29). Between 64 and 67, shortly before his martyrdom, Peter wrote of the Lord's coming and warned believers that "[l]ooking forward to these things," they should "be diligent" (2 Pet. 3:14). Some thirty years later, now that John is an old man, he, too, records in the Revelation that Jesus is coming quickly!

James, Paul, Peter, and John—all of them lived and died without seeing the return of Christ. Indeed, nearly two millennia have passed since Jesus told the disciples, "Therefore, you also be ready" (Luke 12:40). Of course, God is sovereign, free to keep His own timetable as He wishes. When the Old Testament prophet Daniel was given a revelation, God instructed him to "shut up the words, and seal the book, until the time of the end" (Dan. 12:4). But when the moment was right, God's messenger told John, "Do not seal the words of the prophecy of this book: for the time is at hand" (Rev. 22:10). Nevertheless, two thousand years is a long time. Is the time truly "at hand"? What is to prevent us today from being skeptical?

The answer lies in the fact that Christ's imminent return must be defined within the context of "the things which must shortly take place" (Rev. 22:6). Mankind operates in time; God operates in the realm of eternity. Peter, although he expected Christ's return, also counseled fellow believers, "Beloved, do not forget this one thing, that with the Lord one day is as a thousand years, and a thousand years as one day. The Lord is not slack concerning *His* promise, as some men count slackness" (2 Pet. 3:8-9). Note that Peter states that a day is "as" a thousand years to God. Peter is using a figure of speech, not a mathematical equation.

If Jesus' return must be considered within the context of "things which must shortly take place," let us take note of what those "things" are. God's redemptive timetable includes detailed work with Israel and with each believer, along with a plan for the Church and a plan for unbelieving persons and nations. All these plans must be fulfilled before Christ returns. In the redemptive program of God, the "day of the Lord" is the finale; it will come only after the rest of His plan is completed.

You and I do not know the scope of these details. But we trust that God is working all of these things every minute of every day—even right now. So in the broader context of history, Jesus Christ is in the *process* of returning this very second!

Do not be discouraged if you do not know when the preliminary details of His return will be complete. Think in terms of a construction site. According to 2 Corinthians, God is building a house: "For we know that if our earthly house, *this* tent, is destroyed, we have a building from God, a house not made with hands, eternal in the heavens" (5:1). As you drive past a construction site each day, you first see the foundation poured and the shell erected. But once the house is under roof, you cannot see the contractor installing the wiring and plumbing, laying the sheetrock and floors, and adding the finishing touches. But when the house is finished, the occupants can move in that very same day!

Are you ready for that day? John records that there are things we should be doing now in anticipation of "moving day." For one thing, God's servants are admonished to keep the words of this book: "[B]lessed is he who keeps the words of the prophecy of this book" (Rev. 22:7). In contrast, we are sternly warned against tampering with this book!

> For I testify to everyone who hears the words of the prophecy of this book: If anyone adds to these things, God will add to him the plagues that are written in this book. (Rev. 22:18)

This is a serious warning! It is a challenge that applies primarily to the words of the Revelation and secondarily to the entire Word of God. God also warns of the consequences of ignoring His Word in our daily habits and manner of living. When history is consummated, no one will be able to make any more changes. "He who is unjust, let him be unjust still: and he who is filthy, let him be filthy still: and he who is righteous, let him be righteous still: and he who is holy, let him be holy still" (Rev. 22:11). If Christ returned this moment, would you be unjust and filthy for eternity, or righteous and holy for eternity? Think about this question.

GOD'S WORD IS SETTLED

One characteristic of the Bible that confirms its veracity is its complete honesty. Human flaws and foibles are recorded, as are the great examples of godly and faithful servants. David's sins, as well as his triumphs, are fully exposed. Peter's weaknesses are recorded, not just his positive traits. As we near the end of the Book of Revelation, John is faithful to record even his own momentary failures to heed God's Word. First, when the apostle witnesses the joyous marriage supper of the Lamb, he is overcome. John turns to the angel messenger who has conducted him through heaven, "and [he falls] at his feet to worship him."

> But he said to me, "See that you do not do that! I am your fellow servant, and of your brethren who have the testimony of Jesus. Worship God! For the testimony of Jesus is the spirit of prophecy." (Rev. 19:10)

Then a second time, when John had at last seen everything granted to him to see—capped by Jesus' glorious promise to come again quickly—the apostle was overwhelmed. "I fell down to worship before the feet of the angel who showed me these things" (Rev. 22:8). In his great emotion, John worshiped the messenger instead of the Author of the message. Why did he do this?

Perhaps John responded as he did because he was reared in a devout Jewish family and knew the rabbis' teachings about angels. The ancient rabbis venerated angels and assigned various angels to everything imaginable. They named an angel who was in charge of the wind, one for the clouds, another for hail, and others for thunder, lightning, rain, and snow. They concluded, even, that every blade of grass had a guardian angel. Those ancient religionists were as enthralled with angels as are some people today. So perhaps John was influenced by his past learning. But God does not desire for His created beings to worship other created beings. God desires for us to worship Him alone.

John's failure warns us of how easy it is to stray in our worship. In fact, John erred twice. If this beloved apostle could deviate in his worship, even while being enlightened by an angelic messenger specially sent by God, so can we. What, then, is the remedy for misdirected worship? The angel's response to John and to his wrong worship is instructive.

> Then he said to me, "See that you do not do that. For I am your fellow servant, and of your brethren the prophets, and of those who keep the words of this book. Worship God." (Rev. 22:9)

First, the angel corrected John, clearly stating that his activity was wrong. It was outside the boundaries of God's Word. Although the apostle was sincere, the messenger from God pointed out that John was in error. It is to John's credit that he did not become offended, as do so many in our own day when unbiblical practices are exposed.

Second, the messenger offered John an important reminder. Although angels are superior to mankind in many ways, both the angel and the apostle were created beings and fellow servants of God. All of us, you and I included, are created to serve God for His glory. To Him alone belong all worship and honor. Untold millions in our world today have "exchanged the truth of God for the lie, and worshiped and served the creature rather than the Creator" (Rom. 1:25). Even in our churches, often, we pay more attention to the messenger than to the message. Like John, we end up worshiping a fellow created being and servant, rather than the One to whom all our worship is due.

Finally, the angel declares to John the most important lesson of all. When the apostle tried to worship the angel the first time, the angel stated to John that "the testimony of Jesus is the spirit of prophecy." This statement means, quite simply, that the Person and message of Jesus is the essence of all true prophecy. True worship focuses on the One who is Truth! The second time John erred, the angel reminded him that God's servants are people who "keep the sayings of this book." It is the words of the Book that keep our focus on its

Author and drive us to bow before Him in true worship, worship that honors Him alone. This same Book, this Word of God that is "forever...settled in heaven" (Ps. 119:89), declares that the return of Christ is imminent. He is coming again! Since this is so, "what manner of *persons* ought you to be" (2 Pet. 3:11)?

When you and I think of the awesome power of the God who at this very moment is working out His great redemptive plan, our response can be only this: We must recognize His majesty. We must be humbled by His grace and mercy. We must be emptied of self. And we must fall on our faces before our God in true worship.

THINGS TO THINK ABOUT

1. How does the anticipation of Christ's imminent return affect the way you live? the way you worship?

2. How would you answer people who scoff at Jesus' promise to return? After all, nearly two thousand years have gone by since He made that promise.

3. What two ideas (Rev. 22:7, 18-19; 22:11) does John record that will help you be ready for Christ's return?

4. Why did John err in trying to worship the angel? Does his error have any parallel to unbiblical worship practices you see today?

5. Explain in your own words the three correctives that the angelic messenger used to bring John into right worship.

SCRIPTURE INDEX

ABOUT THE AUTHORS

D

r. David Whitcomb is pastor of Community Baptist Church in Greer, South Carolina, a ministry he founded in 1985. He holds a Doctor of Sacred Ministry degree from Northland Baptist Bible College and a Master of Arts in theology from Bob Jones University. Pastor Whitcomb is known for his careful exegesis of God's Word, his commitment to the ministry of the local church, and his heart for training new men in the ministry. Under his leadership Community Baptist Church has grown into a vibrant congregation with a vital testimony in the greater Greenville, South Carolina area. *True Worship* is his first book.

M

ark Ward Sr. is a gifted Christian communicator whom God has used as an author, broadcaster, educator, speaker, and musician. He is author of six books, including two histories of religious broadcasting, and has appeared on numerous national Christian talk shows as a commentator on religious media. Today as president of Message Media Group, Mark is a full-time writer and communications consultant to Christian ministries. He has served as communications director and magazine editor for several national ministries and nonprofit organizations, and taught communications and writing at two Christian universities. A frequent speaker at Christian writers conferences nationwide, Mark serves on the advisory board of the American Christian Writers Association. As a broadcaster he has been producer and speaker for four nationally syndicated daily radio programs. Mark also ministers with the Calvary Quartet that travels throughout the eastern U.S. and has recorded several albums. He is available for church meetings and conferences by emailing Message Media Group at message@messagemedia.us.

ABOUT YOU

This book has explored what the Bible says about worship. One clear principle of worship is that only those who truly know God through saving faith in Jesus Christ can offer true worship to God. According to the Bible, if you *know* God (have a personal relationship with Him), "you may *know* that you have eternal life" (1 John 5:13).

But I am sinful. I have wronged God. How can I have a relationship with the God against I have sinned?

The Bible says that God sent Jesus Christ to reconcile our relationship with Him, "having made peace through the blood of His cross" (Col. 1:20b). This promise is for those who believe in His Son; not a mere belief that He exists, but belief *in* His Son.

Christ died a gruesome death that guilty sinners might be reconciled to God. The relationship that has been broken by sin may now be made right.

What if I don't want a relationship with God? I have my friends. I don't need God.

The issue is much more serious than lacking friends. The issue is that due your sins against a holy God, you are under His wrath. He is very displeased with the crimes that you have committed against Him, and He will justly punish those crimes. The punishment? Hell.

So is that it? Am I condemned forever?

Yes. Unless you admit some things:

I need a Savior. "For all have sinned and fall short of the glory of God" (Romans 3:23), and "your iniquities have separated you from your God" (Isaiah 59:2).

Christ died for my sin. "For Christ also suffered once for sins, the just for the unjust, that He might bring us to God" (1 Peter 3:18).

I need to repent of my sin. "He who covers his sins will not prosper, but whoever confesses and forsakes them will have mercy" (Proverbs 28:13). "Repent therefore and be converted, that your sins may be blotted out" (Acts 3:19).

I must receive Jesus by faith. "But as many as received Him, to them gave He the right to become children of God, to those who believe in His name" (John 1:12).

I can be sure of my salvation. "He who has the Son has life" (1 John 5:12). "Most assuredly I say to you, he who hears My word and believes in Him who sent me has everlasting life and shall not come into judgment, but has passed from death into life" (John 5:24).

If you would like to respond to what you have just read, cry out to God from your heart and pray the following prayer in your own words:

> Dear Jesus, I realize that I am a sinner and that I need a Savior. I believe you are the Holy Son of God who died on the cross to pay the penalty for my sins and bring me to God. I am sorry for my sins. Forgive me. By faith I receive you as my Lord and Savior. I ask that you save me now and grant me eternal life. I now place my trust in You. Amen.

If you have repented of your sins and have believed in Jesus, start out your new life in Him by getting a copy of God's Word—the Bible—and begin to read it every day. Start talking to God in prayer each day; you now have a relationship with Him! And find a church where the Bible is believed, preached, and lived. Attend there as often as possible and look for ways to be involved. These three things are crucial to your new life in Christ.

Let us know about your decision. If we can help you get started in your new life in Christ, or if you have not yet decided to receive Christ and have more questions, please write us at the following address: Ambassador International, 427 Wade Hampton Blvd., Greenville, SC 29609. You may also call (864) 235-2434 or send us an e-mail through our website at *www.emeraldhouse.com.*

OTHER BOOKS BY
MARK WARD, SR.

MUSIC IN THE AIR
Hymn & Song Stories from the Golden Age of Radio

Radio's golden age was an exciting time of great preachers, great quartets, and great songwriters who gave us some of the world's best Christian music. Read the exciting stories of radio pioneers like Charles Fuller; groups like the Old-Fashioned Revival Hour Quartet, the Blackwood Brothers and The Statesmen; and songwriters like John W. Peterson, Mosie Lister, Ira Stanphill, Stuart Hamblen, and others who made the radio days golden.

THE WORD WORKS!
151 Amazing Stories of Men and Women Saved Through Gospel Literature

Ever give out a gospel tract and wonder if it did any good? Now you can find out! How? Through this collection of 151 true stories of men and women around the world who were saved by picking up or receiving gospel literature in miraculous ways. You will be encouraged about your own witness!

SHOTS IN THE DARK
The Sniper, The Suburbs, and the Things We Value Most

In the year 2002, the capital of our nation was held hostage by a new form of domestic terrorism. The D.C. Sniper paralyzed a city of four million people by targeting the things that make suburban life possible—shopping centers, parking lots, gas stations, interstate ramps. *Shots in the Dark* provides an account of the shootings and what they reveal about the things we value.

Ask for them at your
local bookstore or contact:

Ambassador International
427 Wade Hampton Blvd.
Greenville, SC 29609

1 (864) 235-2434
www.emeraldhouse.com